SUCCESS

How I Ended Up Here!

Vernie L. Walker

**(The premier guide to discovering the
ultimate sales person in you)**

SUCCESS

How I Ended Up Here!

(The premier guide to discovering the ultimate sales person in you)

Versie L. Walker

First Edition

Published by:
A New Look Publishing, LLC.
Post Office Box 1111
NY, N.Y. 12533 U.S.A.

Orders@newlookpublishing.com   http://newlookpublishing.com

Unattributed quotations are by Versie L. Walker

Copyright © 2009 by Versie L. Walker

Library of Congress Control Number: 2009904704

ISBN, print ed.

First Printing 2009
Printed in the United States of America

Library of Congress Cataloging–in–Publication Data

Walker, Versie L
Success, How I Ended Up Here! - The premier guide to discovering the ultimate sales person in you / By: Versie L Walker
Includes bibliographical references (p.) and index.
ISBN-13: 978-0-9824271-3-2 (trade pbk. : alk. paper)
  1. Success How I Ended Up Here! --United States.
    I. Walker, Versie Title: Success How I Ended Up Here!

Photo by: David Livshin
Cover design by: Keith Axelrod

CONTENTS

Contents

PREFACE

You will notice that throughout this book I speak of *dreams, faith, beliefs and desires.* These words will be seen repeatedly all through the pages of this book. When using these words, I'll be speaking from my life's experiences. It is these experiences, bad or good, I've allowed into my existence, they have manifested inside of me and enabled me to become the very best that I can be.

These words, *dreams, faith, beliefs, and desires* are the very foundation in which man can only exist for his greater (or **greatest**) good. For me, they have proven to be self-evident when used in their proper context, along with the words "I am." These words "I am" are the most powerful, the most prolific and the highest that one can get. It calls up all of the powers of the universe and all of your faculties and places you in alignment with the great "I am."

What is it that drives you, me, and countless others to head out on a journey far different and far greater than anyone we personally know? What is it that makes you *dream, believe, desire* or have *faith* in something that others can't even conceive? What is it? It is the "I am" that is in you, that corresponds with the universe, each and every time you say it.

The words *faith, belief, dreams and desires* were never new to me. However, I never knew their powers and how they correlated with the universe and our mere existence, until attending Christ Universal Temple/C.U.T founded by Johnnie Coleman. Here they teach truth principles, the universal law of attraction and how we, through positive thinking and affirmations, can change our lives for the better. The power of right thinking and the ability to attract like consciousness into your world and affairs is their primary focus.

Johnnie Coleman went on to teach that, not only can you achieve wealth and prosperity, you can also call up the faculties within your own body to help fight off disease (pronounced "dis-ease") and sickness. It was her teachings that led the entire congregation to believe that they can "Live a Healthy, Happy and Prosperous life."

My visits to C.U.T. came at a time in my life when I was actively seeking change. Hopefully, you are as well. By reading this book, your willingness to apply these principles, this book will assist you in that change.

During one of my earlier visits to C.U.T., I had the pleasure of meeting *Les Brown/Author/Public Speaker*. This meeting was due in part to my friend, now wife, giving me tickets to attend a seminar that he facilitated surrounding his new book. The seminars were held over two weekends. I was overjoyed to be there, to be in the presence of one the best motivational speakers of our time.

As you will read, I have for quite some time wanted to be an inspirational speaker and here was my chance to be up close and personal with one of the best. At the end of the seminar, he would sign his new book, which was included with the seminar package.

Upon approaching the table where he sat, it came across my mind that this could be me.

This meeting was twelve years ago. My *dreams, faith, belief,* and *desire* to do so never subsided.

I look forward to meeting each and every one of you as we travel through life's journeys. I look forward to hearing your stories as well.

Take care.

"I AM."

ACKNOWLEDGEMENTS

To my family, my loving and supportive wife, *Maryann*, "We did it." To my two lovely daughters, *Kendall and Jasmine*, thanks for being my biggest cheerleaders and fans. Continue to *believe* as I have always taught you... *"you are and always will be the best in what you do."* To my son, *Versie III*, I have only loved two men in my life as I do you; they are your Great Grandfather *"the Great James Hopkins"* and your Great uncle *"Rocky"* - both of which you have never met but, I'm sure they are, as I am, proud of you.

To my mom, *Norma Walker*, the strongest woman I have ever known. To you I say thanks; thanks for all that you have done and continue to do!

To my sister, *Andrea (Mimi/TiTi)*, here I go again on a new venture/journey and here we are again together holding it down...I love you!

To my mother-in-law, Betty Sprinkle, who believes in me and continues to support my business ventures.

To all of my family and friends; it's because of you that I have and can do what I do. You have inspired me more than you may ever know.

To my Grandmother (Arlene), you are gone but not forgotten. Thank you for teaching me love unconditionally...I know that you are watching over us.

To my friend Jerry McCarthy, thank you for seeing something in me and for encouraging me to become a Financial Advisor, take care.

To Mr. Marsh and Bobbi Marsh, thank you for believing in my entrepreneurial spirit and for allowing me to piggy back on your *dreams,* "Let's Get Poppin!"

Stop! Before you read any further, upon finishing this book, would you promise to pass on this inspirational book to a family member or friend as a gift? You will be able to order a brand new one, either by faxing the order form located at the end of this book or via our web site at, www.VersieWalker.com or sales@newlookpublishing.com

Don't forget when ordering to use promo code "PassItOn," to receive your new copy of SUCCESS, HOW I ENDED UP HERE! Signed by the author.

As an added bonus for sharing this timely informational book, as a gift, we will include the supplemental guide, SUCCESS, HOW I ENDED UP HERE! A guide towards changing your life.

DISCLAIMER

This book is designed to provide information on sales, sales concepts, and techniques. It is sold with the understanding that the publisher and author are not engaged in rendering legal, accounting or other professional services. If such assistance is needed, the services of competent professionals should be sought.

The sole intent of this book is to provide insight into selling based purely on my personal beliefs and experiences. We urge all readers to review all available material regarding sales and tailor the information to meet your individual needs.

A career in Sales is not a get-rich-quick scheme. Anyone deciding to become a sales professional, self-employed or an entrepreneur must expect to invest a lot of time and effort into it. For many people, being a salesman or becoming self-employed has provided more freedom and proven to be more lucrative, than a traditional nine to five job and many have built solid, flourishing, rewarding businesses and careers.

The purpose of this book is to inform, educate, inspire and even entertain the reader as we review the many facets of selling.

*"Set your mind to what you
want your reality to be"*

--Maryann Sprinkle-Walker
Finance Manager, Wife, Mother

INTRODUCTION

As I began preparing to write this book, I had to consider how to present the material to you, the reader. I am greatly concerned as to how I can inspire you into action. I, a man that grew-up on the north side of Chicago, only a few miles away from one of the notorious housing projects ever, Cabrini Green, and raised in a single parent household. How can I convey the importance of what I have to offer?

I guess, the only way that I know how, *"Straight and direct, that's how!"*

From the very beginning, I decided that this book would not be one of those quick fix books; i.e. 10 steps to success, 5 ways to be rich or in just two simple steps you will have more clients than you have ever dreamed of. That just doesn't work…it does however, sell a lot of books. But it doesn't send the great majority of us on the road to our life-long *dreams* of *success* and *financial freedom.*

For me, sales have and always will be a part of my life. As far back as I can remember, as far back as grammar school (2nd & 3rd grade), I have sold something to someone.

I can recall each week that my mother would give me money to replenish my school supplies (15 to 25 cents).

In the hallway of my grammar school, there stood this huge vending machine and in it were sheets of paper, pens, pencils, rulers, etc... Each week I purchased what was needed.

Soon, I discovered that I was buying supplies more frequently than needed. This wasn't due to my excessive use of these items, but due to the fact that I was sharing them with many of my classmates. I later found out that many of them didn't have working parents and they depended on monthly government funds.

This was my first introduction to supply and demand. I could buy 25 sheets of paper for $.15 or five pencils for $.10, at which time I would sell three or four sheets of paper for $.03 to $.05, depending on the supply, which we all know drives the demand. This wasn't done to capitalize on their misfortune or disadvantage, but I did not see why my mom should support them or why I should go without, because of my generosity. Thus, begins my journey into the life of Sales.

FINDING DIRECTION

At various periods in my life, I encouraged friends, strangers and family members to fulfill their *dreams* and many times I had not followed my own advice. I found myself going from relationship to relationship or job to job searching for true happiness.

In many cases, fighting that true aspect of my nature, the thrill of the chase-sells, either due to its hard work, or the negative connotation that sales may have, or simply yielding to a more certain path, "a guaranteed pay check." Yes, it is guaranteed as long as you work that week or if your skills are up to par and you're not being replaced by new technology.

I have done a little bit of everything:

- Cut hair (self proclaimed Barber)
- Worked on cars
- Sold imitation designer goods
- Worked at McDonalds
- Worked in a factory

I even worked for the Chicago Transit Authority (CTA) as a ticket agent and train conductor. I worked as a Telemarketer (I may have called you). I worked as a debt collector for a company that collected on defaulted student loans (great experience and an eye opener to the world of financial services).

I've partnered with close friends to start up and create businesses. Self studied to become an insurance agent, as well as a series 7 licensed Financial Advisor for several major banks, advising their retail customers on suitable investments. I elected to leave the 9 to 5 and became self employed. I am currently on my third (3rd) business venture as an entrepreneur and enjoying life now more than ever before.

I have done it all. Although many of these jobs are polar opposites of one another, they each have helped to define me as a salesman in one way or another.

In the United States, for the most part, we no longer produce many of the goods we use or depend on. Many of our industries have gone out of business or have been out sourced to faraway lands. As a society that produces nothing and consumes everything, we must rely on the Sales and Service industries for job creation and, in many instances, these industries are one and the same.

First Sales Job

I have had several jobs with the word sales in the title, but was everything but. Sometimes I would simply be a stock boy in the sales department, guiding customers to the isle where they could find the items that were on sale...but hardly a Salesman.

Many times, I even wore the shirts or badges that stated Salesman (more of a service provider than a salesman) but never delving into the true aspect of a salesman/ salesperson role. For all you true Sales people, you know what I mean and I shall elaborate more in future chapters.

What I consider to be my first sales job was as a Telemarketer. I obtained this job with the help of a friend from high school, named Ken. He was one of those guys determined to succeed by all means necessary. In high school, he would drive to school while we all were freezing at the bus stop. He was working at McDonalds while the rest of the guys were trying to see what new party we were going to attend each weekend. By the time I started in the work place (McDonalds), he was working for non-profit organizations.

I'll talk more about him and others that helped to *inspire* me.

For this position, I interviewed over the phone. I was given a small script and asked to read it while being recorded. The interviewer would play back the recording, and then would let you know if you should come in for a face-to-face interview. The process was done in this manner to see if you had the conviction in your voice and voice inflection necessary to prompt a prospect to do as suggested over the phone.

In this position we used headphones to enable us to better hear the prospect. We were provided with a list of prospects to call, and given a script, then placed in small cubicles as an office. The pressure to perform successfully in selling was heightened by having supervisors, and their managers arbitrarily listen to our sales pitch (talk about pressure).

Needless to say, I didn't last very long at this company. I just couldn't seem to make the quota of four commitments from customers per night. I had several of these positions throughout my career. Each time with a little more success, but learning this wasn't the career path for me.

Because of this, I found myself staying away from these types of jobs, or so I thought. Even when I was hustling up on odd jobs or interviewing for more permanent ones, I would find myself having to convince individuals in such a way as to why I believed that I was the perfect candidate for the position.

The ability to talk eloquently was very helpful in finding new sales positions. Unfortunately, merely having an ability to talk knowledgeably about a job or career was inadequate. It was worse for me since I was totally inexperienced in the career paths I had selected. Most of the time, I was simply a fish out of water. But I did possess a burning *desire* to achieve and succeed. For me, failure was not an option.

So, I decided to change my methods. I began to study people, their actions and reactions. I used vocabulary that would ignite and attract. I spoke to their comfort zone or level of understanding. I've been able to have people reveal things to me that their mom or their pastor may never get to hear. They knew beyond a shadow of a doubt that their information would be kept sacred with me. I began to notice I had the ability to get people to open up to me, sometimes total strangers, which then started to feel much like what sales and customer service should be.

Many of you reading this book possess these same qualities as I do. Perhaps, like me, you haven't met your fullest potential. However, as great as these qualities may appear, they are only part of the required package to success. Although this book will help you learn sales strategies, techniques and concepts, it cannot change your personality, character, determination or integrity. An outgoing personality, a strong determination, an insistence on integrity...these are some of the hidden qualities which ultimately will determine your success. It is often said that a winning personality is everything but, that is not necessarily true. It will get you to the gate but, you had better bring a lot more to make it across the finish line as a "winner."

WHO CAN SELL

In theory, anyone can sell anything. An item, a product, or service, but not everyone can be sold. As a salesperson, you must be keenly aware of your surroundings and someone's body gestures. These non-verbal signs can influence the entire sales process. These gestures may show up as folded arms, eyes wandering or even fidgeting. You should pay close attention and respond quickly to them.

Many times the prospects/customers are unaware that they are even doing anything. More importantly, this behavior could potentially be a road block down the line. Either way, addressing it will allow you to move forward.

I suggest mirroring the person with whom you are talking to. If they fold their arms, you should fold your arms, and if they cross their legs, then you should cross your legs. Most times, they wouldn't be aware that you are mimicking their behavior. However, it has been said that doing this gives the other party a sense of comfort (strange, I know).

Noticing and being able to read body language is vitally important. Furthermore, you must move quickly to eliminate it, in order to ever close the sale.

There have been many occasions, where I was unable to read the various body languages of my customers and thereby missed sales opportunities or experienced a high rate of buyers' remorse.

Sales are all around us

In today's world, it is difficult to find an industry, career, or jobs that do not have some aspect of sales as a part of your responsibilities. They are selling you on something, a concept, a way of life, an item either tangible or intangible, on a belief, or a theory. Some sales appeal to your ego. Some sales are a necessity and others are a convenience.

The next time you go to McDonalds (yes, McDonalds will sell you). The first thing that the cashier says to you when you approach the counter is; *"Hi, welcome to McDonalds, may I take your order?"* At that moment, he or she is an *"order taker,"* and the very instant he or she asks *"Would you like a hot apple pie or to super size your order,"* they, unknowingly, have become a sales person.

If you have young children, teenagers in particular, you have been sold more times than you could ever imagine.

For example:

When your loving teenager comes and asks you if he or she can stay out late on a particular school night and you invariably say "No," their comeback may be as follows, "well, since I can't stay out late, you must not trust me (guilt) or since I can't stay out late on a school night, you can at least let me go to the movies with my friends on Saturday."

He or she knew very well that the school night would not fly. They really wanted to go to the movies on Saturday all along but, gave you the *either this or that* sales pitch.

Price Selling

Price selling is where or when the sales person feels that they can only get a person to buy if the display conveys and communicates their prices upfront. These individuals often times feel that they cannot sell or compete in a competitive environment unless they can price match or beat their competitors' prices...Not true, whatsoever. We will be discussing more of this throughout the book.

Take a look at this example:

Hello ma'am, can I interest you in anything today? Yes, do you sell house chargers? Yes we do. Well how much are they? The price is right on the package they are $21.95. The customer replies "$21.95, no thanks; I'll just buy it elsewhere."

A better approach would have been as follows:

Hello ma'am, can I help you with anything today? Yes, do you sell house chargers? Yes we do, do you have your phone with you? Yes. May I take a look at it please (now, with phone in hand, you can control the sale). Yes, they're right here. Let me plug it into your phone to show you that it works. Wow, it does work how much does it cost? They are only $21.95. You said $21.95? Yes, that's not expensive for this type of charger and X Y & Z companies across the way sells them for $10 more. Since they sell them for that much, I might as well buy it from you.

Thanks for your help.

Feature Selling

Feature selling is a term that I like to use. This is whereby the sales person has full knowledge of all the features that a product may have and all of its practical uses. This could prove to be very beneficial in those situations where a customer is looking for something specific, or needs a lot more information to make a buying decision. Even so, I am not a big fan of feature selling; it has its place during the sale. However, it is not the driving component that always closes the deal.

Benefit Selling

It is my belief, as well as other professionals, that I have encountered, that each of us believes wholeheartedly that the sales process will never take place if a customer cannot find benefit in what you are selling (or offering). For the sales person, it makes it twice as difficult to try to sell something with no benefit.

So often, salesmen try to become knowledgeable in all the features available, or try to price compete, to justify why you should buy from them. Let me state, quite emphatically, that *this does not work*. On the other hand, knowing something about the product, your customers and their plans for use of the product, does work and it works every time!

Product knowledge and price competitiveness are critical, but emphasizing the benefits of your product or service can overcome these obstacles. Emphasize a believable point of difference in benefits between your product or service and your competition and the potential customer will become more interested in what you have to say. For example, how often have you gone out of the way to buy something because the service was better or perhaps paid a higher cost for an item or service simply because the atmosphere and service provider went out of their way to make sure you were comfortable. What I am saying is that there is something to this benefit stuff, perhaps more than you have ever imagined and I will provide you with numerous examples throughout the book.

Think about the last time you went to purchase something, a television, lawn mower or automobile. You already had in mind how much you wanted to spend and how much more than that you were willing to go. When the salesperson starts in talking about all of the features, your mind starts to think "cha ching," here we go with all of these extras. You say to yourself, I don't want them and I don't need them, I am only spending X amount of dollars.

Then again, the professional salesperson, that has done some fact finding (more discussion on fact finding in later chapters), may have different plans for separating you from your money. He or she would briefly mention the features and then strongly discuss their benefits.

Case scenario:

Hi Sir, how are you today, can I help you find anything? "Oh," so you're looking for a new vehicle. Are you from the area? *NO. You say you're from* the <u>Midwest</u>, where about? *Chicago.* They say that's the windy city, right? Is there any particular vehicle you had in mind? *An SUV,* we have some right over here. What brings you to the area? *Job relocation,* for you or your spouse? *My wife.* Do you have any children? *Yes, three.* Three you say? *Yes, two girls and a boy.* That's great!

In this scenario the sales person was actively engaging the customer and extracting pertinent information that will aid him later on in closing the sale.

Now, here's an example on how <u>not</u> to present the products!

So, Mr. Walker, you seem to like this model here. Let me explain all the features of this vehicle. It comes with a six disc CD/DVD changer (cha ching), it has heated leather seats (cha ching), there's a power hatch and moon roof (cha ching) - (**an example of feature selling**).

Here's an example as to how it should be done!

So, Mr. Walker, you seem to be interested in this model here. She is a <u>beauty</u> and with all that it comes with, it's a <u>steal</u> at this <u>price</u>. Let me go over all of its features with you. It comes with a six disc CD/DVD changer, for those long drives, with your <u>family,</u> to the city. It has heated leather seats for those cool brisk mornings or evenings. There's a power hatch for ease and convenience of storage.

Lastly, it comes with an alarm and remote starter for just $5,000 more. Think back to any cold day in January back in <u>Chicago</u> (the customer begins to shiver, as he recalls how cold it can get). Now, imagine that you have to shave, the kids are not ready and you have a meeting that you are running behind. Think of how you would have to go and sit in a cold car for ten minutes or so to get it warm, or stop shaving to start the car. Then have it run while you go back into the house, not safe. How about simply pressing this button here, and have the car warming up while you are getting ready and not having even left your house. Now, isn't that worth the little bit extra (perhaps not; however, the sales person showed the benefits of each feature and that's what closes the sale)? - **(an example of benefit selling)**

Types of Service Providers

Customer service providers; these are the individuals that most of us depend on to assist us. They are the ones that we call on and look to when buying something or when having something serviced or when in need of assistance. These individuals are usually well versed in the procedures for getting things done and provide you with immediate answers.

They are normally the first stop in seeking a resolution to many of your questions and/or concerns. Many of them are savvy enough to think outside the box and come up with ways for solving a problem. A well trained and self-efficient customer service department can prove to be a great asset to any business.

Order takers; these individuals are the ones that work in an environment that has high volume calls or traffic. With this group, everything is planned and prepared for them. They're only required to follow the plan as laid out, with no opportunity to alter what is being offered or presented.

Many order takers are located on the other end of the 800 numbers, when you call for the item you saw on the infomercial last evening. This group has no real say or input in the preparation or the presentation of what they are offering.

Many times, when asked specific questions or if they are able to alter or change what is being offered, they're not sure if they are allowed to do so and at times can be heard saying, *"I don't know, I'm only an order taker."*

Salesmen; are the people employed to sell goods or services. Salesmen are there to assist and offer you the various products and services that their employers make available. These individuals may work directly for a company or they can be independent contractors for a company. Some work in an office, some from home, and others travel from location to location, meeting with their customers.

Let's look at an example of two service providers. Two friends work in the food service industry, one person works at McDonalds and the other at Red Lobster...

The McDonalds worker:

- Paid $7 an hour
- Works 35 hrs per week
- Receive 5 to 35 orders per hour.
- Orders range in price between $2.18 to $16.50

- Average orders $9.34 (only illustrative, not actual averages).

- Up sales/cross sale at least 3 products per hour

The Red Lobster worker:

- Paid $2.50 per hr plus tips
- Works 35 hrs per week
- Receive 5 to 25 orders per hour
- Orders range in price between $9.95 to $25.95
- Average orders $17.50 (only illustrative, not actual averages).
- Up sales/cross sale at least 3 products per hr.

Each of the above examples is used to illustrate how each individual would be paid in those scenarios.

Both of these jobs are in the food service industry, but, as you will see, for the same amount of hours and perhaps the same amount of orders, how one is more compensated than the other.

For the McDonald's worker:

- He or she gets paid every two weeks approximately $490 (not including tax and other payroll deductions).
- Roughly $49 a day ($49 x 10, # of days worked in a given pay period).

As for the Red Lobster worker:

- He or she gets paid around $175.00 every two weeks (not including tax and other payroll deductions)
- Roughly $17.50 per day ($17.50 x 10, # of days worked in a given pay period).
- Tips averaging approximately $3.50 per order. An average order $19.89 x 18% tip rate or $3.50. The Tip of $3.50 x 5 orders = $17.50.
- Total tips of $17.50 x 5 hours worked per day are approximately $87.50.
- The estimated tips per day of $87.50 x 10 days = $875.00 per pay period.
- Add the base wages of $175.00 plus the estimated tips $875.00 = $1050.00 bi-weekly or $2,100 per month.

These numbers may vary depending on the time of day and number of days worked. More importantly, you get to see how one could make considerably more money for basically the same type of work.

Now, for the Red Lobster worker, his/her efforts of providing a service instead of being an *order taker*, directly affect their bottom line. He or she walks away with roughly $2,100 per month.

On the other hand, the McDonald's worker earns roughly $980 per month. Here, he or she has no opportunity for additional income for the same hours worked. No matter how often they offer additional items for the customer and no matter how many items the customers buys (no tips here).

This could be the very reason why one leaves work at the end of their shift, waits for someone to pick them up, and go to their parents' house. While the Red Lobster worker drives off in their own car and perhaps go home to their own apartment.

THE AWAKENING

Some people believe selling is a state of *consciousness.* Others believe it is a way of life, a mind set, a systematic pattern of behavior. Not everyone is suited to the rigors of commercial selling. And yet oddly enough, everyone is engaged in selling...they are just not being paid for it.

For example, let's say that your wife sold her girlfriend on the idea of buying an item from a certain store and gave the location, color and sizes available, etc... However, as much as her girlfriend may have appreciated the information, your wife did not receive a dime for her efforts. Not your wife, not you, or your family benefited monetarily from that information.

How about yourself? How often have you made a referral, recommendation, or gave an impromptu testimonial for an item, product, or service without receiving any remuneration? I would submit this occurs regularly with most people. We all give advice, and recommend products or services without a second thought. We might receive some thanks and feel some satisfaction that we have "done the right thing."

We are currently in an economic environment that many people find particularly trying. With the foreclosure of so many homes, the failure of so many businesses, and the total loss of investments by the average individual as well as the unemployment of millions, many are discovering the need for high quality professional services and advice.

These individuals are very willing to pay for your experience, your knowledge, your time and quite often are willing to pay a premium for them. By this, you and your family could grow and *prosper*. As you are already aware, these are financially scary and uncertain times. Shouldn't you and your family benefit from your time and willingness to help others?

Although the economy appears chaotic at this time, most people are hopefully optimistic. There may never be a more perfect time to review the many new ways selling can be used. Alternative fuel, hybrid cars, new ways to burn clean coal and even the rebuilding of our infrastructure as well as the rebuilding or our health care system are only a few areas to consider.

In the months and years ahead, there will be a demand for engineers to design this new technology, a demand for builders to create it and a need for suppliers and distributors along with installers to move the new 21st century forward. But behind all this effort is the growing demand for salespersons to open the path to the end users.

The Plunge

In sales, when you don't insist, (through demonstration) or convey to a customer why they should buy a product or service from you, then they often times leave, feeling a sense of self righteous indignation. They say things like, "I told him/her I didn't need anything, I'm alright" and "I didn't need any one trying to sell me their product or services."

However, this may be the furthest thing from the truth. By demonstrating your product and or service, you can better display the benefits of each feature. Thereby potentially opening a closed mind and closing a new sale. Who knows, you may even gain a loyal customer.

There have been numerous times, whereby, I encountered customers that said they did not need my products or services and after a brief conversation with them, I was able to uncover a need. Sometimes, after speaking with these individuals, they found what I had to offer was quite different than what they had initially thought we sold. This is why probing and fact finding is so important to any sales presentation. It gives each side an opportunity to see if there is a mutual benefit for them, to continue to speak.

I was once at a sales seminar and the subject of overcoming objections came up, and a gentleman asked, "How do you handle it, when before you are able to tell the prospect what you have to offer, they stop you mid-way and say, they're not interested." The seminar coordinator laughed and simply said, "Tell them I don't blame you; I wouldn't be interested either."

The entire group looked around at each other with a puzzled look on their faces as if to say, what is on this guy's mind. We are trying to get sales here, not throw them away.

At that moment, the seminar coordinator began to explain. He said, "You say exactly that and when you have their attention and they say to you" "yah, that's right, now why wouldn't I be interested? You are trying to sell me something, aren't you?"

You then say "well, I wouldn't be interested either, until I had the opportunity to find out more about what is being offered. So, now that I have your attention Mr. Prospect, let me explain to you how I believe we can..." Objections overcome!

Most people are inundated with sales pitches and constant telephone solicitations. A built-in defense mechanism is gradually developed, whereby people tend to be suspicious of anyone who makes any attempt, however legitimate, to offer a product or service. The best response to this problem is what we call *shock and awe* a method of obtaining interest within the first three seconds. This was the late great P.T. Barnum's tactics (the world famous Barnum & Bailey circus). He would find some weird and unusual specimen and *shock* everyone into wondering what it was and wanting to see more of it, and once they did, they couldn't believe their eyes and the *awe factor* set in.

It is your job to find ways to stand out from the crowd. Find something that separates you from your competitor; that special something that makes you unique.

Let's say that you are an insurance producer and you are selling insurance policies. Find a niche market and work that market until you become an expert in that area. For instance, Long term care policies or Medicare supplements. These are two growing areas as we are nearing the end of the baby boomers' era (born 1946 – 1964) that are now in their 50's and 60's; whose parents are now in their 80's and 90's.

Although you may be a licensed insurance agent or broker able to sell all lines of insurance products, becoming an expert in one or two areas is the way to reach success. It is the reason why most physicians are specialists in one area of medicine. You will find it nearly impossible to offer your company's entire catalog/brochure of products. Consider partnering with someone, who may have expertise in another particular area.

No one really expects you to know it all, especially when you are first starting out but, find what you are comfortable with and work it thoroughly. Divide and conquer.

Self Evaluation

First let's take a look at you:

- How do you perceive Sales people or customer service providers?
- How comfortable are you with having to approach people?
- Are you more favorable to having a face-to-face meeting or do you prefer telephone contact?
- Do you have phone-phobia (reluctance to cold calling)?

- Are you more willing to call on someone you currently have a relationship with, rather than someone you do not know?

These are just a few of the questions that we will be going over, as you develop a sense of who you are and begin to transform your *consciousness* while developing the habits that will create the foundation of a true sales professional.

Any bias should be eliminated from your mind. Perception is the only reality. The less reservation you have to change, the more successful you will become.

Let me ask, how excited or enthusiastic are you when it comes to going to work every day or taking on new projects?

- Do you view this task as being mundane?

- Do you resent doing this, so much, that your entire being is disturbed when Monday morning rolls around and the alarm goes off?

- Do you see your job as a means to your end (hopeless)?

- Are you arriving to work later and later each day or rushing to leave earlier day after day?

If so, is this activity noticeable to your employer, or to your mate? Can your colleagues, in house competitors, see the difference in you? Has this hindered your performance but, most importantly, are you suffering?

You should ask yourself: are your customers being serviced to the best of your ability (or receiving the highest quality service possible)?

There have been many times, that I myself and countless others have felt the exact same way as you do (helpless, frustrated, under-appreciated, and over-whelmed) but, you can change all that. There is hope and I am here to help.

Imagine if the professional that you put your trust in behaved in the same manner. What lasting impression would this have on your perception of them? How long would you remain a customer?

The unmotivated salesperson causes severe problems for himself and for the company that retains him. As I have already mentioned, I want to inspire you to your greater good. In motivating someone, you can motivate a criminal and he will continue on his path to criminal activities. I believe, if you inspire him, he can take that same initiative and energy and redirect it and perhaps establish a business informing people of individuals such as himself and how they can safe guard themselves against it. Now, he is no longer considered a criminal offender, nor as a law breaker, but seen as a professional resource and can be compensated as such. The power of Inspiration!

I believe that, after reading this book and practicing (employing) many of the techniques that will be discussed throughout this book, you will find that you have what it takes to be successful beyond your wildest dreams no matter what you choose to do. Dreams have no deadlines.

Turning Within

Most of you are familiar with the world famous Lakers' basketball team, as well as Shaquille O'Neal (Shaq). I recall reading an article once, that while playing for the Lakers, Shaq would practice shooting free-throws, roughly 500 or so. Can you imagine that?

With that much practice, Shaq was, in spite of everything, only a thirty eight percent (38.3%) shooter from the free-throw line. Management wanted more.

He had worked with the likes of Irvine "Magic" Johnson, a big guy who had much success in the game of basketball, Phil Jackson, Bill Sherman and others.

The team decided to contract Ed Palubinskas, President of the National Basketball Shooters Association, to work with Shaq during the 2000-2001 seasons. After studying and talking with Shaq, he discovered that he lacked knee bend and had various other physical and mechanical flaws.

After a great deal of resistance, Shaq underwent a total "overhaul" and began to accept Ed's advice and started to make the adjustment/changes needed to increase his average by nearly one hundred percent (100%). He then became a sixty nine percent (69.4%) shooter at the line, which enabled the Lakers to win more games.

The Lakers' strategy was "genius and difficult" to defend against, aside from having the triangle defense. Now, with Shaq's free throw percentage up, they were bound to win. During crunch time, with the clock running out, Shaq would often be double or triple teamed, also known as "Hack-a-Shaq;" thus, drawing the foul and having him to go to the line and shooting the winning score. I repeat "genius!"

Think of how much greater your life would be; mentally, spiritually, and financially. If only someone would give you insight as to how you can improve your game by one hundred percent (100%). This could dramatically improve your value to your company; thereby increasing your bottom-line (net worth).

Remember, Shaq was practicing hard. However, he was practicing a flawed technique and how many of you are doing the same.

On one occasion, I was watching a made-for-TV movie about the life of the five-time Olympic gold medalist winner, Gail Devers.

In 1988, while training in Seoul, South Korea for the Olympics, Gail had become stricken with an illness (Graves' disease). This debilitating thyroid disorder, had threatened to have her become a double amputee (from her ankles down).

Ms. Devers named the "World's Fastest Woman," now faced with the possibility of having both of her feet surgically removed. What a blow! All that she ever knew, ever trained for, ever wanted all could be lost due to this illness. She was devastated to say the least.

However, she made a decision (see, we all have a choice) and according to her bio, the word "quit" has never been a part of her vocabulary. She decided to fight back and not to accept the option that the doctors presented her with. Gail went on to win more medals and break more records and has become a business woman and entrepreneur.

"When was the last time that you were faced with a life altering decision? What choices did you have to make and what was your outcome?"

There was a lot to take away from this movie. For me, the two things that I carry with me to this very day are:

- Her *determination* to succeed.
- Her ability to *turn within* and *overcome* the greatest of odds.

In an interview in the movie, it was said that "she was able to accomplish so much and win so many races, because she always practiced as if she were in competition. During practice, she would push her chest forward and envision herself breaking the yellow ribbon at the finish line."

Understand that your mind doesn't know the difference between practice and live competition.

Ever since watching that movie, I now employ those same tactics at work, in my studies and my personal life. So much so that, when I take an exam, I envision in my mind the word *"PASS"* displayed on the proctor screen.

I remember when my wife and I were building our home. I would drive by the house daily with my children and walk through the site, showing them their rooms, our kitchen, our living room, etc. This seems harmless enough and for most it would be. However, for me it could have been a disaster. We hadn't secured financing yet. See, for me failure wasn't an option. With my *faith* and determination intact, we were going to live in that house, and we did.

Are you teachable?

As mentioned, in his audio CD *25 Secrets to Wealth Creation*, Kevin Trudeau states that there is a *"teach ability index."* The index states how teachable a person is and if you have "a high level of being taught and a high tolerance to change, you are teachable and very likely to become successful." He went on to mention that there is also a *"training balance scale"* which consists of two parts. One (1) part is *"the thought, dreams, motivation and the desire"* and the second (2) part is *"the doing, action and the physical stuff."*

Trudeau also discussed that all the super-wealthy people employed these techniques and how broke or unsuccessful individuals only focused heavily on one area of the scale. Those people focused on the physical aspect and not on the other parts. He further explains that "90% of your success is not on the physical or on the how. But, on the *"dreams* or your *attitude"* and if you don't change your attitude, it won't matter (Trudeau, audio CD).

I agree 100% with this philosophy. You must have balance in order to grow and become successful.

"If you change your attitude, you can conceivably change the world; a successful life can be achieved based on how you perceive."

"As one thinketh in his heart, so is he"

--The Prophet David,
New Testament, Bible--

THE MIND CONSCIENCE

"As one thinketh in his heart, so is he." I would like to add something to this statement and vary it slightly. *"As one believeth in his mind, he shall receive it in his heart and achieve it in his universe."*

Many of you may already be or *desire* to become entrepreneurs. This can be challenging as well as rewarding...I truly feel that everyone owes it to themselves to give it a go.

As I mentioned earlier, I worked for various companies in numerous positions. I have drawn from each of these experiences to help create my own businesses. I mean everything from our sales strategy to our sales approach, including product placement and product selection, always keeping in mind the audience which we were trying to attract.

One of our businesses was the selling of cellular phone and wireless accessories. This business is very competitive, lucrative and taxing. Especially as we were located in local malls the rents, hours and staff can prove to be fatal to someone who does not possess the *will* and *determination* to work their business.

However small our location may have been, I structured and worked it as if it was a large fortune 500 company. This included training manuals, sales scripts, contact information and time sheets. The cell phone industry itself is constantly self-eliminating and reinventing itself. What may be new today could be obsolete tomorrow. The technology can be hard to keep up with and the demands of the customers can be overwhelming. So, we came up with a reference guide for our employees, to better assist them with the sales approach. Here's an example;

Accessories:

Accessories are not an after-thought. They are a mindset, and for many, a way of life!

Be aware of what you have:

- Continually review the inventory of your store and your overstock.

- Suggest alternatives with every sales opportunity. For example: If you sell a customer a face plate, you might suggest a belt clip, so they can show off their new accessory. By doing so, you will have accomplished two things. One, you gave them the satisfaction of showing off their new phone and 2nd you made two sales.

If you do not load the sale with these accessories, they will ultimately purchase them from someone else ---why not you? By selling the accessories and the basic products, you make life easier for them and for yourself.

Once you begin to keep accessories in the front of your mind, it gets easier and the multiple sales just happen--- virtually no resistance. We knew very well that:

- 60% of accessories are purchased on the first visit
- 30% of accessories are purchased on the second visit
- 10% are purchased from anybody
- Must sell value
- Sell early and often
- Ask open-ended questions; i.e., when did you get your phone? Does your phone get good reception?
- Keep it real---Don't over-sell
- Bundle together other products or services
- Overcome objections
- Restate benefits

Tips:

With any sales position, especially cellular accessories, it's not necessarily what the customer says. It's the questions that you might not be asking! "I certainly believe that you can hear. But, are you listening." Ask the right questions.

Lifestyle: Is the phone for business or personal?

Other phones: Do any other family members own a cell phone? Children, Spouse, etc...

Mother and Father: Why not buy for them?

We don't have that: How about this, or let me show you this?

A question for all you sales associates; how serious are you?

How much do you know about accessories or your business?

How much time are you spending each day becoming more knowledgeable about your industry?

How familiar are you with:

- Faceplates
- Headsets
- Car Chargers
- Cases
- Phone models etc…

Cases/Pouches: How about presenting these items this way. You know, you are going to be carrying this phone for the next year (or two). Have you given any thought to protecting it from dings, drops and scratches? The warranty certainly protects you against manufacturer's defects. But the phone can take a lot of punishment in a pocket or purse or just bouncing around in your car. These items can be far less expensive than your deductible.

Car Chargers: There is always the chance that we will forget to turn the phone off at night or we decide to run an extra day, before recharging. If the next day is a busy weekend, with a lot of errands to run, it's no fun to hear the low battery beep, when we've got more calls to make and you are stuck in traffic!

Headset/Ear pieces: With traffic being what it is, it's always a good idea to have both hands on the wheel, for the unexpected stops or lane changes. For example: truck drivers, and mothers with several errands to run; (mention that most state laws require the use of hands-free devices), etc.

Here are more techniques that I used in the cellular accessory industry but, they can be applied in whatever industry you are in.

Wireless Accessories - Techniques & Methods to Highly Effective Selling

Accessory sales should be the norm...not the exception!

Why Sell Accessories?
Accessories are good for the customer

- Makes products easier to use.
- Can enhance the performance or usefulness of the handset.
- Personalize their product to suit their taste or express something about themselves.
- Upgrade the product they just recently bought or enhance an old product they've had for a while.
- All of these increase long term customer satisfaction.

Why accessory sales are good for our company

- Satisfied customers tell their friends and return for future products.

- Accessory sales are high profit products that can impact the bottom line of a company's profitability.

Accessory sales are good for Sales Associates

- Satisfied customers and good word of mouth will bring you more business! You want your customers to say "Ryan at Accessory Land really took care of me; I would recommend you go and see him when you need anything for your phone."

- Customers will have a stronger commitment to do business with someone who understands all of the benefits and options that are available to them.

- Customers are looking for instruction on how to best utilize their phone. **Sales associates, who can offer solutions, will gain more business!**

The Basics

1. **Know your Accessories.**

   - Product knowledge is critical and it's what separates you from the 8-foot wall of accessories in Wal-Mart.

   - Become familiar with each item that you offer.

Fact #1 - *Features* "Tell" and *Benefits* "Sell." Each item has *features* that differentiate it from other similar items.

The fact that the features are more attractive or more expensive is not what sells. The part that *sells* is how the added features of a product will *benefit* the customer. What will it do for him or her?

2. **Know your Customer.**

    -   Keeping in touch with the consumers' demands and their needs will increase your accessory add-on sales.

    -   Familiarizing yourself, with how and where most customers use their phone, will also increase sales.

Fact #2 - 80% of wireless phone use is while traveling in a vehicle. Customers need car chargers. **Most of today's phones only come with a travel/home charger.**

Find out quickly what type of phone user your customer is:

-   Is their phone for occasional or constant use?
-   Business or personal?
-   Will they use it in the car? While traveling?
-   What accessories have they used in the past?
-   How do they prefer to carry it?

Fact #3 - People buy with emotions and justify with facts. Buying brings satisfaction and happiness for a variety of reasons. Your customer may be happy from just getting a raise, angry over a spouse's purchase, or feeling low. A customer may not plan on spending extra money but, if they find a benefit to them, they will buy.

3. **Know your Phones.**

- Become familiar with old as well as new models.

- Know the numerous manufacturers, their styles, features, and model number sequence.

- You need to know what comes with the cell phone. When the customers approach the store with a newly purchased phone, You should ask;

  1. Did the phone come with a carrying holster?

  2. A hands-free ear bud?

  3. A basic car-charger or wall charger?

- Be familiar with the tons of distributors and wholesalers. Know who they are and where they are located. Know which items they carry and at what prices.

This information is key to helping effectively sell a customer additional accessories other than the ones that are included with the phone.

Fact #4 - Modern handsets are more than just phones. They are cameras, MP3 players, video game systems and even full-blown information managers (PDA). Keeping the batteries charged is vital. Vivid color screens, videos, music, games, and web browsing all drain the phone's battery at a rapid pace. You might want to ask the customer if they are happy with the battery life of their current battery. Their answer just might prompt you to a quick battery sale!

- Understanding compatibility will allow you to demonstrate your expertise and suggest upgrades that allow the customer to get the most out of their phone.

For example: There are several types of hands-free connections:

- 2.5mm universal jack
- 2.5mm jack wired for Samsung on/off
- Nokia
- Jabra C150 Nextel push to talk
- Jabra C250
- Jabra EarWave(Boom &Bud)
- Plantronics /Motorola Bluetooth

4. **Presentation and preparedness help your sales.**
   - Accessories can be an impulse buy if displayed attractively.
   - A customer's first impression is how you, your products and your selling area look.

Maintain a clean and organized work area during non-high volume times and throughout the entire day.

Focus on a neat and clean display. Use the broom and dust pan to pick up debris.

5. **Attitude is everything.**
   - So, you know your products, you know the industry and you know the phones. Now, you

have to know your customers and get them enthused! Have a positive attitude and show enthusiasm. The customers will sense it and gravitate towards it.

- Humor, laughter and excitement are fun to be around. Keep it to a minimum and keep in mind your **GOAL** is to make multiple sales. So **FOCUS.**

Fact # 5 - Did you know that your ears continue to grow your whole life? If we lived to be 200, they'd be dragging on your shoulders. Now, you have a reason to help them find a hands-free headset that fits their size of ear. You could explain that "Many customers find the foam buds pop out easily-usually right in the middle of a call.

Then, you can talk about new hands-free items that may have improved sound quality. They may not feel that they have anything invested in the "free" headset that came with the phone. The same is true for suggesting a carrying case, even if the phone comes with a holster. Many customers like them because you get better protection when (not if) you drop your phone.

You can see that a lot of thought and energy went into training our employees on the importance of appearance, the customers, product knowledge and overall presentation.

I then created an easy to use "Five Step" sales approach to be used at each and every sale. This time-tested, tried and true sales technique is called:

"The Five Steps to Success"

These "five steps to success" can be used at any level of sales and during any sales presentation, regardless of what is being sold.

The Five Steps to Success

1. Greeting: How are you doing? How's it going? Or simply; are you looking for anything in particular?

2. Qualify: What kind of phone do you have? Do you have it with you, and can I see it? Please.

   • REMEMBER, NO PHONE, NO SALE...YOU MUST BE IN POSSESSION OF THEIR PHONE TO CONTROL THE SALE.

3. Show Product: Show the specific item that the customer may be looking for. Reminder, always place the item(s) on or near their phone, remember that customers are visual buyers. Lastly, always show/mention two or more additional items that we have for their phone (up selling).

4. Compliment: Make references to how well the item looks, fits, and feels etc...

   • ATC: (Attempt to Close). Statements such as these, "Would you like to go with this one or that one?" "Is this the one you want or that one?" "Will you be buying one or two?" "Would you like for me to leave the item(s) on?"

5. <u>Close/Ring up:</u> Okay, so you want this one; let's go ahead and put it on for you!

It is extremely important for you to understand the sales process. You must communicate with the customer throughout the entire sales process. This means that during the greeting, during installation and while ringing up the sale, from beginning to end.

It has been proven time and time again, that if you follow these five steps each time a customer approaches, your sales will increase and your success will continue. As you can see, we took our businesses seriously and tried to cover all of the bases.

Always remember, HAVE FUN!!!

You must all understand that sales are sales, no matter where you are and what you are selling. From widgets to humongous earth moving equipment, you must bring a certain philosophy to sales. You must possess the basic fundamentals of the sales philosophy and have the mindset that you want to achieve a stated objective. Then, after acquiring the terminology and product knowledge for that particular area of sales and using the various techniques that I have brought fourth throughout these pages, you will find that converting *suspects* into *prospects* and prospects into *customers* is far easier than initially thought.

TYPES OF BUYERS

Conscious and informed

Conscious and informed;   Are those customers who have done their homework, shopped around, read the consumer reports, did price comparisons (with the use of the internet or right on their cell phones) which makes the buying process simpler and easier than ever.

These individuals can prove to be your friend. They can prove to be very difficult to deal with. They know exactly what they want. However, they can be the most loyal and provide solid referrals. If you have what they want, you can generate continuous business even if your competitor has better prices. With these individuals, you must be up-front, honest, and quick to respond to their needs. They truly appreciate the Sales professionals that are knowledgeable of the products, features and their competitors.

Needs-based Buyers

Needs-based buyers can be difficult. These customers have a need, either real or perceived. These individuals only want that item or service to fulfill that need. Usually, they can't be persuaded to an alternative and if you don't have what they want, they will not wait for you to get it. They will simply move on to someone who does. *Not really loyal.*

These type of buyers have a need brought on by loss or damage and just prefer to have it replaced (even if there are new or better products available) with their same item. These buyers can be abrupt or rude. They may just ask "do you have this," and should you say no, they will simply walk away.

I found the best remedy for these types of buyers is to take possession of their product (if applicable) and then engage them in conversation (fact finding) about the product, asking what they particularly enjoyed about the item and the length of time they may have had it.

Doing so will better position you to transition into a sale of the exact item they are looking for, or to a suitable substitute. Selling to these customers can be rewarding. But, many times the sales experience is frustrating. Unlike the conscious buyer, they only give you one chance to get it right. *Not a real good referral source.* You are only thought of should the need arise.

Impulse Shopper/Buyer

Impulse Shopper can make a "bad day good" and a "good day wonderful." They are more pleasant to work with and less pretentious. If they walk pass your business and see something that catches their eye, they will avail themselves to you.

These shoppers usually have family members, friends or acquaintances that are very much like themselves.

They are very loyal and can become a wonderful source of referral business. They generally buy a lot and very often.

"Sales are in the air"

The new global world is more real/evident than ever before; but not very apparent for most. With the Banking and insurance industries in crisis, the collapsing mortgage industry, along with the threat of potentially losing one or more of the three major auto manufactures. Americans are finding themselves having to make some very tough decisions.

With all these massive changes, new sales opportunities are emerging every day. There is a new President with a new administration, with new agendas and new ideas. There will be a need for someone to create more efficient processes, someone to sell their concepts, distribute their product, bring them to the market place and sell the products to the public. Where will you be in the scheme of all this new growth and opportunity?

Remember. Be mindful and very aware that, in sales, communication is key, verbal and non-verbal. It is essential to understand what the customers are saying and what they may not be saying; as well as how you respond to each. This point is critical to the sales process and your success.

When selling you must:

- Be decisive.
- Be assertive.

- Be creative.
- Be proactive.
- Be honest.
- Speak clearly.
- Annunciate.

Several years after becoming a Financial Advisor, I was in a training class that was covering how to overcome objections. I remember the trainer asking for an example of how we would respond to a rebuttal from a potential customer. The prospect did not want to purchase one of our guaranteed investment products. I volunteered for this demonstration, with me giving the presentation and the trainer being the prospective buyer.

After giving my presentation, the trainer (prospective buyer) said that she was uncomfortable with the investments and that she didn't like insurance companies. Upon hearing this, I immediately responded with one of my prepared responses, *"why not, all of your other major assets are insured by some insurance company."* Once again she stated that she had no interest in placing her money with any insurance company and if that was all that I was offering, then we had nothing further to discuss.

Needless to say, I was stumped. I felt that I had the perfect rebuttal buster for this type of response.

The trainer said that my comeback was good. Conversely, I never asked the question as to why she felt the way that she did. I just jumped the gun, saying how all of the other possessions she had were covered by insurance. The trainer went on to say, "Had I asked the right questions,

I may have discovered that after years of her mother paying her life insurance premiums, that upon her death, what they thought she had for final expenses wasn't enough to cover her burial." Plus, how their family had to borrow money to cover the additional expenses and how this greatly embarrassed their family.

I then discovered how, in many instances, I may have lost other sales because of this methodology. Thanks to this lesson, I immediately changed my sales approach.

This brings to mind a story that a friend of mine sent me from my days in the banking industry. She said to me that "This sounds like something you would say." The story is of a young salesman that was disappointed about losing a big sale, and as he talked with his sales manager, he expressed grief over losing this sale. He explained "I guess it just goes to prove that you can lead a horse to water but you can't make him drink." The manager replied, "Son, your job is not to make him drink. Your job is to make him thirsty."

Wow, how profound is that. You must get the prospect wanting the product or service so much that they are compelled to buy.

Sales Techniques

Pausing is perhaps one of the easiest and most effective of strategies. It can be used before accepting a proposal. It leaves the proposing party wondering if they offended you or if they should offer more. It can also be used in rejecting a proposal. It gives the party being rejected a sense of comfort in your decision. Perhaps, you had to really think it through before coming to such a decision or you may have had some inner turmoil while having to come to such a difficult decision.

Using this technique before you close a sale or answer a question can be fatal or could solidify your sales. Pausing too long appears that you are indecisive, uncertain, or on the other hand, move or speak too soon and you appear insincere or anxious. Either way, timing is everything. When used at the precisely right moment, this technique could give the appearance of great deliberation, focus and control.

Selective hearing is the process of delaying, ignoring, or not responding to negative comments until you have finished with your presentation. Many times during your sales presentation you will be able to answer questions with a simple demonstration of the product or service.

There was one time, while working with one of my employees, a customer approached asking for directions to one of our competitors. This employee paused. He then looked the gentleman in the eye and said, "Pardon me what did you say?" The man repeated the question of where XYZ Company was located. My employee began to posture. I was pleased…until, out of this employee's mouth came the *words "Right there, behind you."* He knew better, this man hadn't asked where Sears was. He didn't ask for the rest room. He specifically asked about our competitor. This was unacceptable.

I then approached the man and merely said, "Sir, are you looking for anything in particular?" He said, "Yes, I'm in need of a house charger." I said "We do have it." The man responded, "Great, because I hate dealing with XYZ Company. You saved me a headache." Immediately, we gained a new customer, and a sale.

After that transaction, I spoke with that employee and he gave me every excuse as to why he did not handle that opportunity differently and I shot each one of them down. I explained to him that we have less sales and revenue due to that very behavior and attitude. I went on to explain to him that the month before we were down $3,000 and that I could see why; based on that sale and others like it.

Example

- *$21.99 (price of product)*
- *x 2 (the number of missed sales during a shift)*
- *x 2 more (the number of shifts per day)*
- *x 30 (the number of days in a month)*

These amounts total up to $2,639 before taxes. Very close to our realized loss for the month prior. He was amazed as to how I was able to break it down so precisely. I then asked him how long could he survive with a $3,000 dollar reduction in his income and, as you may imagine, he didn't have much to say.

In this situation, opportunity knocked twice. Has this situation ever happened to you? If opportunity did knock twice, were you better prepared to take full advantage of it? Perhaps, but not likely, if you haven't recognized nor admitted to your mistake, unfortunately, you will probably unknowingly continue missing these types of opportunities.

We all have shortcomings. Just how much have you and your family suffered from them.

More of these techniques are covered in the section *How to Qualify a Prospect or Lead.*

Speaking Techniques

Language is the key to success in many cases. How and what you say is pivotal to making the sale. The type of words used in your presentation must be aligned with the culture and vernacular of the prospect.

In sales, the appropriate wording is essential. It can change opinions, solidify relationships and cement deals. How you frame up your words, along with your body gestures, can paint a vivid picture.

As a rule: in retail sales you may wish to stay away from saying things such as;

- All we have...
- All that is left...
- We only have these...
- It may work...
- I don't know...

However, if you were selling the very last two tickets to the Super Bowl game and you used any of the above mentioned words, they would work.

Undesirable situations require more creative ways to help overcome sales resistance.

In Portland, Oregon, in one of the malls where we were located, I noticed one of the Cingular (AT&T) workers making a lot of sales, while her co-workers were not. Many of her co-workers were there complaining that they couldn't make sales and how the customers had bad credit and they may not meet their sales quotas. Many of which were concerned about their jobs (after observing these individuals and seeing how they carried themselves, they had reason to be concerned).

There was one young lady who appeared unusually successful while her co-workers seemed to be struggling. I asked how she was able to find success while others around her were failing. Here is what she told me.

While she is working with a customer and sees that they have a particular phone that they are interested in, before going any further and wasting her time and theirs, she would ask if she could run their credit.

Once their credit came back, no matter what the score was, she would behave in the same manner (cheerful and positive). If their score came back unfavorable and the company required a deposit, she would say, "Great news, you've been approved and once you put down the required deposit ($100, $300, or $900), we can finish up the paper work and you will be on your way in about twenty minutes."

She said, "Versie, do you understand that most of these people already know that they have credit issues and most of them can't even get a home phone. So, by me being upbeat and positive, they feel a sense of accomplishment. For most of these people they've been turned down elsewhere or were told a much larger deposit would be required."

This young lady found success by having a different perspective. She achieved higher sales figures than her co-workers and had no fear of her job being in jeopardy.

What are you saying and how are you saying it?

Much can be said about those who have mastered the Kings' English. Throughout the dawn of time, many of the great leaders, pastors, politicians, and romantic figures, have been some of the greatest speakers and writers of all time.

These individuals have been able to captivate and delight their audience. They've been able to inspire others to move into action. They have had the capabilities of having others do as they wish.

These individuals have written laws, created businesses, and prepared speeches. They have been able to start and end wars and they've created some of history's greatest moments in time.

The greatest speakers, orators, poets, leaders, and statesmen of our time, all have been able to invoke a great deal of emotion through the spoken word. The way you talk can enlighten; it can demean, encourage or can destroy a sale.

Many of the great speakers of the 20th century (or of all times), were not always very well educated or versed. Most of them did not use big elaborate words to convey their message. For many, it was the manner in which they spoke and delivered their messages, which made them great.

The manipulation of language has opened a new genre of speech.

Through the use of Hip Hop style music, the music recording industry has increased a million fold. In just the past 10 years, it has escaped the perils of Urban American and landed smack dead in every corner of the world.

Many of the music industries pioneers and newcomers have been able to take everyday words, and accompany them with a string of similar words in order to paint very vivid pictures of their life. These pictures can be as grim as any of Steven Spielberg's movies or as triumphant as the fall of the Berlin Wall.

Here is an example of word usage and how the same sentence can be interpreted differently:

1. *"Sheila,* can you come over this weekend?" Here the sender wants the individual to know that they are speaking directly to them.

2. "Sheila, *can you* come over this weekend?" Here the sender wants to know about the receiver's availability.

3. "Sheila can you *come over* this weekend?" Here, the sender wants to know about her capability.

4. "Sheila can you come over, *this weekend*?" Here the sender is stating a specific date or time.

Or saying;

1. I love you.

2. I *love* you?

3. I love *you*!

Each of these statements has a very distinct meaning. One could be a term of endearment with no true intent. The other could be a question as to whether or not the sender is certain of their statement, and the other, a testament to the world as to how one truly feels.

The great romance novels throughout the years have skirted around these words, I Love You.

They have communicated every other aspect of life to indicate those words and feelings, but never actually committed to them. They have said such things as:

- A rose by any other name will smell as sweet...
- You mean more to me than life itself...
- Life without you is not worth living...
- Your love is timeless and I will cherish every moment...

All of this "beating around the bush" to avoid those three lovely words; I LOVE YOU. I must admit, it does make for great story telling.

I have challenged many of my colleagues, employees, friends, and now you, the reader, to find different ways to communicate your thoughts, feelings, and ideas.

Communication can be very challenging. In our society we are constantly searching for new and improved ways to communicate. Often times, the difficulties are felt during non-verbal methods of communicating. With the explosion of the information super highway, i.e. cell phone, texting, and internet e-mails.

Since the advent of these new methods of communicating, the receiving party can easily misinterpret a comment or statement for something other than its intended purpose. Here, you are not able to either see the recipient's facial expression or hear their voice inflections; thus, making this popular and convenient method of communication difficult.

Furthermore, there is a need for everything to be politically correct. It makes me wonder, with all of our education and advanced technology, why do we find ourselves communicating worse than ever before.

Statements

Statements can be misconstrued or confusing to others, either stated or implied. Understanding during communication depends greatly on the thoroughness of the one speaking. Vague statements and not being exact or specific, when advertising or speaking, can leave others uncertain as to the full intent of your statement.

I caution you to be very precise when speaking with customers. You will find that statements made during sales are almost biblical. Take the time needed to go over the various aspects of the product(s) or service(s) being offered and go so far as to ask if they understood what you have gone over. Leave nothing to chance.

For example, if a customer were to ask if they can return an item and you answer yes, you had better be very specific, if your company's policy allows for full return or exchange only within a certain amount of time, accompanied with a sales receipt, etc.

Unfortunately, in the retail community, customers want everything and will play on your omission, intentionally or otherwise, to get what they want. You cannot assume that they will think rationally or act reasonably.

Sales Strategies

My sales strategies/approach can be used in any industry, no matter what it is. These basic fundamental approaches of style, behavior, ideals (ideologies), and attitudes can be utilized effectively in your professional as well as your personal relationships.

If you would commit to following the steps that I have written/outlined throughout this book, you will find success beyond your wildest imagination. These approaches to sales will enable you to sell during low periods, slow economic times, and throughout the seasons.

I believe that your products and services should always be at the forefront of your customers' minds. Your customers are buying your products; why not from you!

This brings to mind two successful Real Estate agents. One I had the pleasure of meeting, the other I've heard about.

Recently I scheduled a meeting with a client that I inherited as a Financial Advisor. The purpose was to introduce myself and review her investment portfolio. She was a small yet powerful woman, who at the time was somewhere in her 70's, with 20 plus years of Real Estate sales experience.

I asked her how was she able to stay in the real estate business so long, with the business being so competitive and basically, from what I could see of her portfolio, she had done quite well for herself.

She explained how she was a stickler for time management. If clients saw a home they were interested in, she wouldn't meet with them right away. She would have them answer a series of questions (qualifying them) and then research her data bank of listings to see what was available that would meet their criteria, all without leaving her office.

After gathering this information, she would then contact the client with three or four listings for them to consider. After a day or so, she would call them back and ask if they were interested in any of the recommendations she had given. If so, she would then meet with them and drive to the one or two properties they had an interest in.

This woman outsold her colleagues year after year and for ten years straight was the number one sales person in her office. She managed to have less down time and virtually no, no shows. She had a system. Her strategy was not to utilize her e-mail for long continuous correspondence. She called or e-mailed you once or twice, after which time she had enough information to know if you were a serious prospect, deserving of her time or not.

The other sales agent would show her clients several homes. Upon finding two that were of serious interest, she would drive them back to the one they appeared to favor the most. Once they got out of the car and approached the steps, she would pull a Polaroid camera from underneath her front seat, and call out to the client(s). Once they turned around, she would snap a picture of them in front of the home and before parting ways she would give the photograph to them.

This strategy was very effective in her closing large sales, much like the car dealer that lets you take the vehicle home for a test drive, or the old Shop owner on Main Street, any town in America. The owner on Friday's would let the kid, who kept coming to his shop to stare at the doggy in the window, take the dog home. The Shop owner, knowing full well, that the dad wouldn't have the heart to bring the dog back on Monday.

The act of having a customer want something so badly that he or she will take possession of the item before they actually own it. This was and still is one of the most creative and effective strategies in closing a sale; nine times out of ten, the customer will close the sale for you.

In case you missed it, these individuals each knew their markets. They had a system and did some sort of fact finding. Without it, you are dead in the water.

Every great professional develops a system, strategically placing themselves in a wining situation; it only makes sense. Why go into a situation blindly, only to discover that you can't help the person or that they are not sincere prospects. "Time is money" and how valuable is your time?

In sales, always remember that you will never be successful if you are "selling tomorrow and not today." This means not selling a product based on the assumption that some better style or color may come out tomorrow.

Realize that consumers are a fickle bunch. They already feel that something new or better may lie ahead. It is your job to convey (especially if you have something to their liking) that what you have may very well be all there is. Often times, allowing a customer to dictate a future sale, will lead them ultimately back to the original or similar option that you presented. Unfortunately, many times it's with your competitor.

Limiting Options

Limiting Options is also an effective sales strategy. Too few choices or options, and the customer may become dissatisfied and not act. Too many options and the customer may become overwhelmed and not move to a favorable decision. Knowing your customer and asking the right questions up front, will help you transition smoothly to a sale.

Finding the right number of options to offer a customer might be difficult at first but, after having done your fact finding, you will be able to decipher quickly as to what type of customer you are dealing with. With practice, you will have this down pat.

I know of some shoe salesmen, who, after bringing out several boxes of shoes and sensing that they have an uncertain buyer, would go to the back room and stay an excessively long period of time, only to reappear with a totally off item (different style or type than what had been viewed previously) or returning empty handed, stating that the shoes shown were all that they had left.

Doing this forces the customer to make a buying decision, based on what has already been presented, and many times they pick the very one or two items that they had initially looked at.

This may seem unorthodox but, by removing additional options, you cut down on lost time and opportunity, thus making the customer commit to a decision. We do it in relationships all the time, by removing all the so-called options. We then concentrate on what's in front of us and begin to appreciate what someone may have to offer.

Retrain yourself to view every "sales opportunity" as your last opportunity. I understand that, in order to stay in business we need and want future sales, but allowing it to be at the sacrifice of today's, or this month's sales goal, is far too costly. Tomorrow will come. When it occurs you will be able to take care of the inevitable tomorrows...today.

Business owners and managers recognize that stale stock or an over abundance of inventory, in today's fast paced environment, can kill the business. With today's sales outlet, no matter what the industry, if there is inventory involved, they must move every unit possible with a sense of urgency.

These businesses and their owners are in need of revenue (cash flow). With the tightening of short and long term lending from banks, at this time, businesses must have positive cash flows for payroll, rents, shipping, inventory, etc. This will allow them to not only stay open, but also, to meet with current demands.

How to Qualify a Prospect or Lead

When meeting or speaking with a prospect or lead, you should use open-ended questions when qualifying that prospect or lead. These are questions that cannot be answered simply with a one word answer, for example.

- *How old are you*: *answer 21.* A better way of phrasing this would be; *when were you born*: *answer, March 13th 1954, it was said to have been raining that day.*

Another very effective method is the *feel, felt, found* method of qualifying a prospect, for example:

- Mr. Lot of bucks, I understand exactly how you feel; many of my customers felt the same way as you, but what they found once they met with Mr. Walker was that the information he has was of value to them (or, of great benefit…or very informative)…so, let me have Mr. Walker speak to you.

Another highly effective prospecting and qualifying tool is the: *"How do you mean"* method.

When a prospect gives you a response (excuse) and you want them to justify it or expound on it, this method can get you a lot of mileage and help to close the deal. Many professionals use this approach, even psychologists. Example:

- The prospect says I *don't like XYZ person, store, city, etc.* You simply look them in the eye and say *"how do you mean?"* When they respond, with no change in your demeanor, you ask again *"how do you mean?"* This works with both negative and positive responses and you can use this 10 times with the same person, if it is delivered correctly; they will never know that you are using this technique.

- Using the *"I see"* method works just as well as *"how do you mean"* this method can be used in conjunction with any of the other methods mentioned or simply by itself.

Throughout the chapters of this book, I will discuss the various strategies, tactics and behaviors needed to become a dynamic sales professional. You will discover the various stages of prospecting, customer profiling and steps that every sales person should know, that will help you close 80% of all sales opportunities.

After reading this book, you will better understand what obstacles you can eliminate or overcome, to become one of the most sought after or revered professionals in your field.

For starters, if you change your associations, your mind set, and your habits, invariably you will change your life.

I encourage you to read this book (perhaps over and over again) and "take charge of who you are and who you really want to be."

Continuous Prospecting

Prospecting never stops, it is ongoing and continuous process. Even if a lead is given to you and said to be pre-qualified, you should always follow the steps of pre-qualifying them yourself. This will save you a lot of time and headaches in the future.

In many cases, especially where others are receiving compensation or rewards for referring, they seem to always inundate you with poorly qualified leads. They simply hand the referral over to you and expect you to close them. If you find that this is the case, immediately talk with that individual and make sure that they know exactly what you are looking for in a lead.

Furthermore, provide them with a guideline or criteria and instruct them that, if they find someone that fits these criteria, they should then feel very confident that their referrals won't get rejected and everyone is happy.

Prospects also become disenchanted with being shuffled around from desk to desk, or made to sit for hours, waiting for an appointment. It is particularly discouraging to discover that the person they waited to see was unable to assist them. A simple Q and A would have resolved the issue at the start and avoided the embarrassment and loss of their time.

"Change and growth are a work in progress," understand, "you must put in the work in order to progress."

--Versie L. Walker,
Author, Entrepreneur, Salesman

LIFE CHANGING

Change is inevitable. It is the one constant and it is constantly changing. Change, and rapid change, will affect the way you work, play and prepare your life. It will either be imposed on you or you can impose it on others.

It was in the summer of '93' when my world as I knew it, would change, turn upside down, literally. I had for nearly two years been considering a career change and periodically kept in touch with a high school friend of mine. Each time we saw one another, I would notice how he had prospered materially and financially. It was always good seeing him and each time I did it made it crystal clear that I was not meeting up to my full potential. I was not challenging myself and therefore wasn't being rewarded financially.

We had spoken one summer's day and decided to meet later that evening and chat about the business he was in. I was truly in need of some direction. Shortly after we got together, we went out to a popular area where the youth of the time would hang out and show off their cars and motorcycles. It was there when we both decided to be wild (really a first for me). We decided to race and were warned to only race in one direction, because in the opposite direction there was a curve that had proven to be too much for most to handle. Initially, we followed this advice. However, we couldn't resist the temptation of coming back and racing in the opposite direction.

This would be my moment of truth. I could not handle the curve and I wiped out. I still remember seeing my buddy's break-lights as a blurred streak of red lines swerving around the curve, as he spun out of control in front of me.

I vaguely recall hearing him yelling at his girl friend as they were rushing me to the emergency room, "keep talking to him, and don't let him fall asleep." I could hear his tires scraping the wheel well of his car as he sped over bumps. Much of what happened after that is a blur but, I do recall him saying to me at the hospital, "You must be loved." He stated that he had made one phone call and in 15 minutes there were 20 people at the hospital, all concerned about my well being and how he felt that it would take twenty calls to get just a few people to come and see about him (a moment of clarity).

Due to this accident, I suffered head trauma, shoulder injury, stitches in one knee and staples in the other. I was in bad shape and fortunate to be alive. I can still recall hearing one of the nurses in the operating room say, "Breathe young man breathe, doctor his is not breathing, breathe young man."

It was during the time of my recovery that I studied for eight (8) to ten (10) hours a day. I would read the various laws and practices of being a debt collector. This is why we had met on that summer's night. He would introduce me to his world, the world of debt collections (I was clueless). This was not my area of expertise. It was at this time however, I found strength, the strength to go within and discover a new me.

In my physical condition, I needed the assistance of my loved ones for virtually everything, which was a very humbling experience.

There was one particular day when my sister was taking me for a walk, to help strengthen my legs. This was the first time that I realized that I had been running fast and going nowhere in my life. I suddenly asked her to stop. She immediately became concerned. She thought that I had become exhausted or perhaps was in pain. I explained, "No, I am ok, but listen to the sound." She said "What sound" (seeming very annoyed). See, I <u>used</u> to joke a lot and she was very serious when it came to me and my well being. "Those sounds, the sounds of the birds," I said; "the smell of fresh cut grass, see how amazingly blue the sky is?" I was now seeing life through new eyes. My sister believed that I had lost my mind!

Sometimes, life has to knock you down, in order for you to look up and then to get up. Sometimes, your greatest victories are born out of your lowest points or toughest challenges or most trying times.

The Challenge

After being immobile and studying for an entire month, I had a scheduled job interview as a Debt Collector. On this same day, was also my first doctor's visit to begin rehabilitation for my legs (there was no opportunity to reschedule either appointments). The pain of this first session was so intense and so excruciating that I believe I may have blacked out once or twice. I remember yelling at the Nurses and at the Therapist.

They insisted that this had to be done now and in this manner in order to help separate the scar tissue and for me to gain full movement of my legs. After which, I was still in a tremendous amount of pain and I refused any pain medication. I got dressed and headed to my car. A simple two minute walk took me ten minutes and took just as long for me to get in my car.

I drove my car two miles to the expressway, where I sat at the top of the expressway's entrance with tears rolling down my face. I had a decision to make. If I turned right, just two exits away and in less than ten minutes, I would be home. If I turned left, I would drive for 45 minutes towards a new world, a new beginning that I knew nothing about. I knew that if I went home, there would go my opportunity for change but, if I went left, would I be given a chance or even be ready for that change. I decided to go left and my life has been transformed forevermore.

It is during these times that we discover who we really are. It would have been easy to go home and be comfortable and safe. I probably would have gotten a lot of sympathy and support had I done so. However, after that accident, I was no longer satisfied with being comfortable.

Ups and Downs

Being a Sales professional requires the ability to endure the ups and downs of selling. The peaks and valleys of selling must be met with a discipline and focus that eliminates the depression during the valleys and the hubris during the peaks.

Many times, Sales professionals experience brief success and celebrate it (celebrating often times too long) and do not document what it took to get there. During the low periods, they spend too much time dwelling on it and without a time tested track record to draw from; quite often, they continue the behavior that keeps them on a cyclical/repeated cycle of ups and downs.

This emotional roller-coaster is not good for anyone. It will tear families apart. It will keep you on a probationary warning with your employer, and prevent you from obtaining your personal and professional goals.

"Stop the madness, get on the right track." Keep good records, have a set schedule and a format as to how you will proceed with each day and task. Do not deviate from your stated agenda or goal, monitor what is working and eliminate what isn't. During the high or good times, continue to do what is easy and working. So, during the low or trying times, it will not have such an impact on you.

As I tell my children, who would prefer to only do what they enjoy, I say to them as well as to you, *"do what you have to do now, so that you will be able to do what you want to do later."*

You may recall me mentioning my days as a debt collector. It was during my 3rd month in the business, when I simply deviated from my script. Not intentionally, but I did. It was the week after the Labor Day weekend that the Department of Education (DOE), for which the company that I worked for had a contract to collect on their defaulted student loans. The DOE sent out a series of dun letters to all of their delinquent defaulted student loans.

On the following Monday, I arrived to work early and was met by the front desk receptionist urging me to get to my desk, saying that we have a ton of calls coming in. I jumped right into action. I had so many contacts and promises to pay from those calls, I was sure to have the best month of my life. By mid month, I had nearly four (4) times the contacts needed to see a commission check in excess of $25,000, not bad for only three months in the business and also recently promoted to supervisor. By month's end, I had the worst month since starting there. I was frustrated, angry, and looking to quit.

A few days later I spoke to my friend, who helped me get into the business. I was complaining as to what a horrible month I had and how I should consider looking for another job.

He calmly asked me to go over step-by-step what occurred during the month. Right away I began to defend myself and stated that I did everything that he taught me, explaining that it wasn't my fault (ego or ignorance). He asked again, so I gave him all of the particulars. He immediately discovered the problem and told me that I did not follow the script.

He was able to identify where I went wrong. I relied too much on the calls coming in from those letters and hadn't verified their addresses, their contact information, or anything that would ensure future excess to those individuals.

I was under the assumption that, if they got the letters and called in, we must have all current information. Wrong, many of those letters had been sent to old addresses of friends and family members that had access to these individuals. So, once they received this official document, they urged the individuals to call in.

He knew the business and provided a sense of relief. This never happened to me again, no matter where I moved. No matter what the job entailed, I did not deviate from the script I created. I had learned my lesson.

Charting your progress

Chart your progress immediately. Starting today, jot down each step you find to be successful. Examine this chart to pinpoint exactly when or if you begin to fall short.

During the highs/peaks, chart the activities that contribute to your success:

- What did you eat?
- How was your mental health?
- How was your home life...new home, new baby, etc?
- Did you arrive to work early or stay late?

- Was there a goal set, either personal or professional?

- Were there any incentives available, bonuses, trips, etc?

These questions may appear strange but, you will find that they contribute to your personal and professional success.

Now, during the low/slow periods/valleys:

- Was there any personal distraction?

- Any professional distraction, such as a change in personnel, modification in payouts, job losses?

- Are goals not being set?

- Lack of time and priority management, checking e-mail and voice-mail during prime business hours?

- Low or no prospecting effort?

Many of the things during this period you have control over and some you may not. However, you must try to stay on course and follow your objectives especially prospecting.

Prospecting for customers is essential to any sales position. You must prospect continuously anywhere and everywhere. Each time you make a sale, you have lost your best prospect and now you need to find three more. This means you need time to cultivate new relationships, (not everyone will buy from you or at least not right away) to replace that one.

During the time I was a Financial Advisor, I would prospect daily. Even though the bankers would give me leads and we had quite a few walk-ins. I took the initiative to find clients on my own. This should be your set routine:

1. No checking mail or voice mail between 9am to 5pm (unless it's during lunch time).

2. I would make no less than 100 calls per day.

3. No calling seniors during the hours of 11am to 3pm (they were never home during that time, they are out running errands or socializing), they are a very busy group.

4. I made sure that two nights per week I did late night calls until 8pm.

5. No calls to residents between 5pm – 6pm (working people are not home, they are on the road).

6. My weekly appointment goal was for 18 set appointments knowing that 17% or three (3) would cancel.

7. Saturday calling was a must to catch those individuals not around during the week days. Saturday appointments were usually the highest number of cancellations.

This activity, coupled with referrals and walk-ins proved very profitable for me and allowed me autonomy and freedom.

Be sure to speak with some of the people at work who seem to find success, month after month. *"Be careful, a winning attitude can be contagious."*

If you notice someone achieving success and seem unorthodox in their approach or immoral, use your better judgment as to what you will take away from these individuals. *"Believe me, you can learn from the best and the worst of people."*

DETOXIFICATION

Detox; *short for Detoxify; -n.* **1** *short for* **Detoxification***,* **2** *a section of a hospital or clinic for drug or alcohol* **Detoxify***;* **1** <u>to remove a poison or poisonous effect from (something).</u>

When having the discussion about success, or fame and even wealth, many people are afraid to try to attain them. They will routinely use numerous excuses, as to why they have not achieved the amount of success they know they should have. They'll even bring up stories about someone they know who had tried this or that and had failed (*toxic*).

For many, it is much easier to talk about what could have been, than what should have been. You will find more naysayer's at the water coolers than you will find progressive minded people. Laziness and procrastination will prevent you from reaching your optimal best.

There are millions of excuses and probably as many people, who use them:

- I'm too old.
- I need money to start.
- I wish I had done it years ago.
- It's too late.

- I have kids.
- I have too much going on.
- I never finished school.
- I know someone who tried and they failed and they are a lot smarter than I am (wow, very *toxic*).

I am certain that you have either said these same things yourself or heard others saying them and perhaps much worse.

With this much poison circling around them, it's no wonder why so many people feel unfulfilled.

There is probably one major excuse that has prevented more individuals from ever reaching their goals, or achieving their hearts' desires.

Would you like to know what the number one excuse is? Or why people haven't changed their lives? Why they haven't taken control of their destiny? Why they have settled for "less than their best?"

Do you really want to know the very words that have put more people in a perpetual cycle of mediocrity, frustration and poverty? Are you interested in knowing those very words that have prevented men and women alike, from seeing this great nation of ours? The words that have sent more potential doctors, teachers, builders, scientists, philosophers, and yes, even writers, to an early grave?

Those two little words; the same two words which have stopped powerful men just a few yards away from the finish line and prevented so many others from ever suiting up.

I am very apprehensive at this moment, just at the mere thought of mentioning these simple words to you. For fear that they might prevent you, as they have so many others throughout the ages, from achieving their dreams.

Unfortunately, I now must share these words with you. I have to caution you, asking that you use discretion as to how and when you should use these words. Personally, I say never. But, I will let you be the judge.

These two words that I speak of are small but yet very powerful words. Here they are:

I CAN'T!!!

Yes, these two simple words, "*I can't*" have stopped more men from being Kings and more women from pursuing their dreams.

I ask that you *detoxify* yourself of these words, the attitudes they may cause and the destruction that they bring. Replace them with, the words, "*I CAN*" and believe me, you will!

EMPOWERING

Sales can be the great equalizer. It evens the playing fields.

For those that may have been or felt disenfranchised from main stream culture. For those who may not be Rhode Scholars. For those of you without family wealth or influence and for those without a great amount of athleticism, Sales can prove to be successful, by the way of riches (money in the bank), property, peace of mind (priceless) and also social status.

In many sales positions, you are able to win praise and recognition amongst your peers. As well as industry heads across the globe. In some industries top salespeople win exotic trips and getaways, awards, bonuses, etc. Many of these individuals are furnished with company cars, cell phones and laptops and are reimbursed for many of their expenses. There are many instances where, top sales producers are making more income than their supervisor and managers.

The average sales position salary is around $80k, with the low end around $25k and the top at or near $150k. There are many sales reps, depending on the industry, after you tack on commissions, bonuses, sales incentives, trips and reimbursements, where these individuals' actual earnings are well in the area of $400k plus.

Perhaps you can see why I chose this topic. There are so many possibilities for the truly determined individuals. You can have the financial freedom and prosperity you desire, "The American Dream!"

Enablers

Enablers are those words that people have heard used, or said to others that promote positive thinking. These words carry an encouraging connotation or optimistic tone.

People tend to act or act-out as they have been termed or phrased. In observing people, I've noticed how some individuals speak to or about their children or loved ones and watch how they conduct themselves.

For example:

I once noticed how a father spoke to his child; she was *"sweetheart," "honey," "precious," etc*… and this child acted with a degree of confidence and self-esteem. On the other hand, I have seen the effects when someone speaks disparaging to their loved ones or child. For instance, I saw a lady yelling at her very young child saying words such as *"dummy," "stupid," "and you won't amount to anything."* You could see the child shut down and begin to act out in the manner that they were being treated.

We must use positive and uplifting words to calm our spirits and provide the foundation for positive thinking. Speaking positively must be done both when speaking to or of others and especially when speaking of ourselves. *"You are the words you speak."*

If you go around saying to the world:

- *I'm just an old…*
- *I feel bad.*
- *I can't ever be or…*

Then, you have willed it to be so and it shall be. However, if you were to say:

- *I feel exuberant today.*
- *Hi neighbor, you are a wonderful person.*
- *I am great and I have limitless potential.*

You will begin to feel this way throughout the day and will hold yourself up to the standards that your words have projected.

Here are some enabling words that I suggest using:

Optimistic	*Alive*	*I will*
Helpful	*Brilliant*	*I Can*
Encouraging	*Dazzling*	*Convinced*
Up	*Luminous*	*Sure*
Upbeat	*Positive*	*Assured*
Vibrant	*Bright*	*Certain*
Lively	*Cheerful*	*Spirited*
Vivacious	*Confident*	*Assertive*
Exciting	*Rosy*	*Confident*
Pulsating	*Can*	*Poised*
Energetic	*Command*	*Dynamic*
Effervescent	*Drive*	*Will*
Happy		

And the list continues.

Try adding some positive, right thinking words of your own.

_____ , _____

_____ , _____

_____ , _____

Appearances

Appearances are important in any job, whether you are communicating with a prospect over the phone or face-to-face. Over the phone you ask. "Yes, over the phone!" How you dress states your perception of who you are and how you feel about yourself. It doesn't matter if the person can see you or not. You can see yourself. If you are pleased with what you are seeing, that pleasure will come across the phone lines during your presentation.

No matter what field you are in, dress to impress, dress for success, and look and feel polished. This goes a long way in telling the story of who you are, long before you have a chance to open your mouth. If you are a blue collar worker and wear a uniform, make sure it is cleaned and, if possible, pressed. Those of you in the corporate sector coordinate your outfit, polish your shoes, men try a new tie. Believe it or not, a short sleeve collared shirt is not a dress shirt. Long sleeves please and add a French cuff if you will.

You must maintain your public image at all times. This means having your nails manicured (ladies, short and natural is the way to go). Men, keep your hair cut and be shaved. Women, your hair should be styled and clothes tastefully and appropriately worn. A strict grooming regiment is very essential.

Let your appearance be your business card and have your presentation become your brochure. You will find quite often that people will have no *"questions when they clearly can see, that you are the answer!"*

Transformation

I have provided you with some great information based on my knowledge and experience thus far. Now that you have this information, what will you do with it?

I once read that, *"Knowledge is not information, its transformation."* So, how will you transform your mind and way of life?

To begin with, I would strongly recommend that you look within and thoroughly analyze what is stopping you from moving forward. What are the deterrents? What are the distractions? Have you noticed potential hindrances to your growth?

In this way you come face-to-face with these issues and begin to eliminate them. This may mean less contact with long term friends, maybe distancing yourself from toxic family members, and releasing yourself of all other vices.

Remain steadfast and unwavering in your quest towards success.

Thinking back, I recall the time when I was self- studying to become an Insurance Agent. I created a large banner

t in my room. I wanted to see this banner
hen I laid down to sleep and every morning
e up.

On the left side of the banner was a picture of a mansion.
On the right side was a picture of a yacht, and the center
was a caption that read:

*"Do just enough and stay a slave or do just a little more and
become free."*

It was those very words which became the driving force
behind me. It also became the message that I shared with
others when fear or procrastination immobilized them.

These very words poured through my soul. They
made it crystal clear for me to see why so many of us
are not prospering. Why so many are living unfulfilled,
dissatisfied, and worsening their circumstances. A good
friend of mine says that *"it's foolish to think you are going
to continue doing the same thing and end-up with a different
result."*

We all have become so accustomed to doing the very
minimum required or *"just enough"* and thinking that
we will somehow find freedom and happiness. In all
actuality, doing just enough has placed the great majority
of us on the outside of the bubble, out of reach and out
of touch.

Doing just enough has made us slaves to our life styles,
our paychecks, our surroundings, and oblivious to our
true potential. Continuing to work in this manner will
lead to depression, and false moments of euphoria that
will then subsequently lead to further depression.

This cycle of doing just enough will leave you feeling unworthy, insecure, inadequate, and soon despondent. You may become distant with those closest to you, for fear that they can see through your façade. You must resist this. You must place yourself in the best position possible to receive all that life has to offer. You have the power to change your outcome by simply *"doing just a little more."*

During a hot summer's day in Chicago, while working at CTA (Chicago Transit Authority), I was heading back to work to complete the second half of a split shift. You work four hours in the morning, off for four hours, and then you return to work for the remaining four hours.

I drove down what is known as the "Magnificent Mile," located near downtown Chicago. This is where the finest shops are located and the elite go to enjoy the city. While stuck in traffic, I looked out the window and noticed a middle aged male standing in front of the Gucci store. He was at least 6'5", slender build, hair slightly gray and holding his small dog. He had on linen pants, a Versace shirt and what looked to be Ferragamo saddles. Looking like a Ralph Lauren commercial.

As the traffic began to move ahead, I couldn't help thinking of this gentleman. He looked prosperous and appeared carefree.

This image stuck in my mind the entire ride to work. His image was one thing. But, what I couldn't seem to get out of my mind was how this man was able to stand there on a Wednesday afternoon without a care in the world (so it appeared), while I was rushing to work. I began to think, what he must do for a living and what must I do, so that I could one day have my carefree "Wednesday afternoon."

It was at this time when I decided to "*do just a little more*," so that I may one day have that same type of freedom. Free from worries, free from stress, and the freedom to choose. This made me become focused.

In "*doing just a little more*," you can alter the course of your life. It takes nothing away from who you are and what you may be doing. Conversely, it will add much more to your life.

As an example, getting to work every day just 15 minutes earlier or staying 15 minutes later, you avoid traffic and the parking lot congestion (less frustrating). By bringing your lunch every day, you avoid the long discussion with co-workers on where and what to eat. You save time and money. Paying a little more on your credit cards or paying them off each month will give you peace of mind (financial freedom). Complimenting your mate more often will give your relationship the boost needed for you to pursue your dreams (priceless). Just a little more can gain you more of what life has to offer.

"Faith without Works is Dead."

--John,
brother of Jesus

PURSUING YOUR DREAMS

In Chicago, there was a radio personality named "Crazy" Howard McGee. He got the name "Crazy" from his relentless determination to become a radio personality.

It was said that he would show up at the radio station for a year, every single day, asking the general manager to give him a job.

This guy was determined to say the least. From what I heard, he even told the general manager he would work for free, which I believe he did for a short period of time. To this day, I still don't know whether or not he went to school for broadcasting. Nevertheless, he went on to become one of the top radio personalities in Chicago. Now you should ask yourself:

- What are you willing to do?
- How far are you willing to go?
- What will you give up to achieve your heart's desire?

As for myself, I have sacrificed so much in the pursuit of my dreams. The quest for success is a long road and for many it's not always worth the sacrifice. You must truly want better than what you are receiving, and feel that the price, is worth the difference.

Role Play

Role play is vitally important. It gives you the opportunity to go over what you know, to become knowledgeable of the products, and familiarize yourself with the material.

Role play is essential to a salesperson and a presenter as well as a Broadway stage performer. Just as workouts, practice drills, and conditioning are essential to athletes. It is the place where the average go to become exceptional and where mistakes can be made and corrected.

There is an old saying that "amateurs adlib" whereas "professionals use a script," and those professionals with scripts do as many role plays as needed to appear flawless. There is no truth to thinking that on game night or when it's show time, you will fall in line and deliver the performance of your life-time. This will not happen.

I suggest role playing with a colleague. You can role play with your significant other and you can even use a mirror to role play. In fact, a mirror is a wonderful tool for role playing. You can keep a mirror at your desk. Use it when you are having face-to-face meetings or when you are on the phone.

This method allows you to see your expression as you speak (see what the person sitting across from you sees). This ensures that you're sending out the right message. In telemarketing we would always look into our mirror before a call and say "smile before you dial."

Scripts/Talk offs/Sales Pitches

You've heard me talk a lot about using and sticking to a script, throughout these chapters. The first script you will probably receive will be from your respective employer. Some will allow you to modify it to better fit your style. While others want you to follow it word for word. Either way, you are lost without one.

Initially my scripts were long and full of product features and some quick reference rebuttals. Over time, becoming more familiar with the products, services and the customer base I shorten it. Now I stick to my script. Haven't you seen a poor actor deliver a brilliant masterpiece, due in part to a great script?

If you are in some sort of telephone sales or telephone communications, I suggest standing during your talk offs. This allows you to be focused and your voice to project in the proper pitch and tone. You will have better command of the individual's attention on the other end and you will appear authoritative and confident. Also, during your sales pitch, the customer will invariably interrupt you time and time again. Stay on track. It is their job to deter you but it is your job to deliver the message.

Script Preparation

Script preparation: this process may take a little time to come up with and develop. However, it is critical and without one, others will be critical of you.

A script indicates preparedness. It demonstrates a sincere effort to display professional accountability. A well prepared and well written script will leave nothing to question. A good script will cover all the bases.

In developing your script, write down and highlight the features and benefits of what you are offering. Then narrow down those *attention grabbers,* and be sure to mention them up front. In sales, this should never include the price. Then, practice your delivery.

With any script you will rework the original content. You will have your basic outline/format and from there you can make adjustments as you deem necessary. Always refine your script to cater to certain groups or the times. When selling to or addressing:

- Couples
- Individuals
- Elders, Seniors, or Mature individuals
- Businesses
- Large groups
- Seasonal promotions, etc.

Simply put, know your audience and be able to adjust to suit the occasion.

Appointment Preparation

If you must set and meet scheduled appointments, you have to set aside time each day to prepare for this opportunity. Pull files or documents to support the meeting. Create a presentation piece, either on power point or your company's presentation software. Schedule it in as part of your daily routine along with your other daily activities.

I recommend having a check list of the items and materials needed for various meetings and or appointments. You can start by outlining what is needed for a:

- New appointment
- Current client
- Follow-up
- Cold call

If you have Assistants, train them as to what is required. Have them place a copy of the outline inside each of the folders to ensure that everything necessary is enclosed.

There is nothing worse than having an appointment that you set a week or so ago, show up on time or better yet early and scrambling to gather the information. You want to discuss. You start out with the odds being stacked up against you.

I, personally would always prepare a file folder with all the information I needed and place it in my file cabinet in the order in which I was to meet each appointment, i.e.:

- 10:00 o'clock appointment with Mr. and Mrs. Baker would go towards the front.
- 11:15 appointment with Mrs. Johnson and her daughter would be placed behind the Bakers and so on and so forth.

When I traveled to see clients, I had a traveling file holder in my car that I would stock with all needed materials. On weekends, I would inventory my bins and would replenish them as needed.

The one good thing about this system is, if the appointment doesn't show (a new client). You can discard the presentation piece. Then reuse the folder with its standard documents for the next opportunity.

Commission Structures

Commission structures vary to some degree or another depending on the industry and the sales managers. However, the effects are still the same, "compensation for productivity."

There is the "Straight *Commission payout;*" also known as commission only. It is the payment method often used with sales people. With this method of payment, the sales person is paid a percentage of the sales he or she averaged for a given time period. The commission can be a percentage of the company's profits. No sales, No commission.

The percentage of commission paid is typically based on specific sales targets and goals which are set by management. Sometimes, the sales people are able to set their own targets, but the percentage amount received normally wouldn't change. Simply put, you will receive a certain percentage of what you sell.

For example, if you:

- Sold $2,500 worth of goods per week, every week, this would equal $10,000 worth of sales for the month.

- Your commission is 6%.

- Company pays a, commission check monthly.

- Then, you earned $600 ($10,000 x 6%) in commission for that particular month.

Draw is another payment method used to pay sales employees. Often times, this commission structure is used to help the sales person stay afloat as they build their business. This particular method is advancement against future earnings (*commission*). Your employer expects you to bring in a certain number of sales and based on that number, they will pay (*draw, or draw down*) a fixed amount in anticipation of those sales.

The fixed amount is considered the sales person's annualized salary and is typically offered for a short period of time (3 months). In some cases, the draw's indefinite, provided that the sales person maintains certain minimum requirements outlined by the company.

For example:

Let's say that you had a sales quota of $2,000 per month. Then, $2,000 would be drawn against your anticipated sales (*commissions*) and then paid out to you.

If you were to exceed your sales quota and earned say $2,800, then you would receive the additional $800 above your $2,000 draw. If you were not able to meet your sales quota and let's say you only made $1500 in sales, then you would owe $500 back to the company, which that amount they may or may not roll over to the next month.

Some companies have a forgiveness (forgivable draw) program, and it's where any losses in the prior month are not carried forward to the new month. You will start off with a clean slate. Customarily, this is only allowed for a certain amount of times during a specific time frame (1 occurrence per quarter) before probation and or termination.

Commission plus Salary; is where a person has a stated or fixed salary, independent of a sales quota, and opportunity to earn commission. If they sell any goods that their company offers, then they would receive a commission (percentage of the sold item). Many employers use this method when trying to move certain items or give an incentive to their employees without committing to or locking in to a pay increase.

Offering commission and draws or salary plus commission as opposed to simply having a fixed salary, is a way for employees to be monetarily rewarded for placing maximum efforts in their work.

You will find that there are various industries where commissions are used, including but not limited to: car sales, real estate sales, insurance and investment sales, and a whole host of other sales jobs.

Commission sales are, to me, "one of the greatest inventions ever." I do support the concept of "team" and being a team player. However, in every group, there are or will be slackers. In a commission environment, the true super stars are able to shine and can be rewarded handsomely for their efforts.

Some of the highest paid individuals are commissioned sales people. I glanced at a real estate magazine one day and saw these gorgeous high priced properties (5 to 12 million dollars). 23 out of the 27 names and photos of sales reps to contact for more information were middle aged women. I was glad to see this. It confirmed in my mind that sales are not just a male dominated industry as television would have you believe.

Women make up a good percentage of the high paying sales positions in the United States, from careers in marketing, pharmaceutical sales, bio-tech industry, luxury automobile sales, real estate sales reps, recreational vehicles, and travel agents. The list goes on.

More and more women are paving the way and proving that they not only have a place in this industry, but also, they have staying power. In an article written by Marc Ransford for Newscenter paper, Mr. Ransford wrote that "women may be better suited to handle sales positions than their male counterparts," (Ransford) according to a Ball State University educator.

According to Ramon Avila, the George and Frances Ball Distinguished Professor of Marketing said that recent studies "found that some females have better selling skills." "Many women are more nurturing, have stronger listening skills, and empathize better than males (Ransford)."

Another article that I read, Top Sales Career for Women, by Bill Baker, discussed some of the demands of sales jobs. How it is "highly competitive," and that "a sales job involves lots of hard work." He also states that "in spite of all the tough things that this job demanded, it is in demand for the rewards potentially available (Baker)." Avila, says "Gone are the days of the public telling jokes about salespeople and the horror stories of door-to-door selling" and that "women see sales as a tremendous opportunity because of high pay and rapid advancement (Ransford)."

I know most never envisioned yourselves working in Sales. Many of you probably went to school to pursue other careers altogether different than Sales.

Perhaps, you saw yourself as a large corporate executive, a college professor, and maybe starting or managing your own business. For some of you, you may have seen a sales position as being temporary, until your dream job came along. Well, let me tell you, it's here!

A career in Sales could give you the income of a corporate executive, the rewards of a college professor, and the freedom to come and go as a business owner.

There is a side of the sales industry that maybe unfamiliar.

I have hopefully shed some light on the opportunities afforded to sales people, the unlimited income potential as well as the freedom of being able to schedule your day around your personal and recreational activities.

Financial Advisors and Insurance agents are paid by the organization based on annual production. They may have an Assistant that sets their appointments, prequalifies leads, and finalizes paper work.

Sometimes, the Assistant's job entails handling the follow-ups and answering general questions. This enables the Senior Representative to focus on the more important aspects of the job. This tends to generate higher revenue. I've seen how some representatives have been able to double, if not triple production and greatly increase earnings.

For the majority of sales people paper work is tedious and we will usually pay someone considerably to take over that task.

Distracters

Are you being distracted by your surroundings? Are you more engrossed in minor setbacks than you are in creating and looking for opportunities? Are you allowing yourself to be the victim of circumstances, (or falling into the excuse rut)? You may find yourself saying things such as:

- *It's raining out, no one is coming in.*
- *Its Christmas time, no one is home.*
- *It's slow and I have had 3 appointments cancel; I may as well go home early.*

Use your time effectively, become familiar with product knowledge, and outline the benefits of each product and its features. During slow periods catch up and follow up on leads, paper work, tracking methods, prepare for reviews with old clients, and scout for new ones.

Have you created a circle of influence? Those individuals from your community, old associations, neighbors, etc... These are the people who have "been there and done that" and can assist you with getting that. Are you telling everyone you meet or speak with, what you do for a living and how to contact you should they find themselves in need of your services?

Have you gone back to old leads that had not bought from you? Perhaps their circumstances have changed (new baby, promotion, inheritance) since the last time you all talked. Are you asking for three to five referrals every time you meet with someone, regardless if they buy from you or not?

Think of all the possibilities available to assist you in having great sales, day after day, week after week after week and month after month. Honestly, these suggestions are no secrets. They are simply what the top producers do week after week and month after month.

Top producers usually can't sleep thinking of more creative ways to reduce the amount of "no shows," low sales and how to increase their income, all at the same time, enabling them to have more leisure time.

This will happen for you too and you're well on your way to meeting your goals.

Progressive Selling

You will find that there are numerous selling styles and techniques. I will go over just two that I have found very helpful and that have been highly effective when dealing with customers.

The first approach is the *Progressive selling approach.* This is where you approach the person/customer/prospect very straight forwardly in person or by phone.

Example: (face-to-face);

- Hi, how may I help you today, or are you looking for anything in particular?
- May I be of any assistance?

With this style of selling, you do not wait for the customer to come and seek you out. Once you realize that they are in your store, you provide them the courtesy of acknowledging their presence (progressive approach). When done right and with precision timing, you will find that the customer is very receptive and will gladly accept your assistance.

Example: (over the phone);

- Hi! Mrs. Jones, this is Steven Smith with XYZ co. I'm giving you a call for X reason and would like to provide you with Y and Z. Should I put you down for one or two of Y and Z? (There should be no pausing or asking questions of the individual that would prevent you from getting out what you wanted to say).

This approach typically places you in control of the sales call. Often times, you will have no resistance from the prospect as to what you are offering. Always stay confident and deliberate as to why you are contacting these individuals. You will find that, most prospects are very appreciative of the call.

If you want the prospect to take down your name and phone number or to write down a confirmation number, ask them to do so. Ask that they get a pen and paper and let them know that you are willing to hold on while they get them.

This is neither intimidating nor threatening to the prospect. You are simply letting them know that you have valuable information, and wish them to have it.

I have discovered that more than 45% of sales never materialize because the salesman never got around to asking for the sale. They ask for everything but the sale!

Frequently, sales people give great sales presentations. They will have a customer teetering on the brink of accepting all they have presented. But let it all collapse. Most of these sales people are frightened or have not discovered the secret to *closing* a sale.

Suggestive Selling

Suggestive selling is where, the customer is buying or purchasing a product or service, the sales rep will offer additional products or suggest an alternative to their initial choice. This can occur during the initial interaction with the customer or during the close.

With suggestive selling, you can direct a prospect to do what's in their best interest, example:

- *"Yes, Mr. Smith, you have fallen behind on your payment schedule. However doing nothing will be more harmful to you. There are alternatives that are available. May I suggest..."*

These techniques can also be used during your initial encounter with individuals, example:

- *"Can I help you find anything?"* *"Oh no **I'm just looking,**" (this statement is notorious in retail sales) "okay sir/ma'am, if you need anything, I'm right over there. By the way, we also offer xyz" (state at least 2 – 3 items that may not be apparent or in the customer's view).* Then, simply walk away.

Speaking of progressive and suggestive selling, it blew my mind years back when I was making flight reservations and the reservationist asked, "Will you be staying with family or friends when you arrive, or will you need a hotel?" I said "no" family or friends in the area but "yes," I will need a hotel. She then said "Hold on while I transfer you to the hotel reservationist." After setting my hotel reservations, that reservationist asked, "Will you need a car or will someone be there to pick you up?" I said "no," there will be no one there to pick me up. "Yes," I'll need to rent a car and she said please, "Hold while I transfer you to car rentals."

Wow! One call, the right questions and ten (10) minutes later, I was on my way with no worries.

Overcoming Objections, the "NO's"

In every aspect of life *"No's"* are inevitable. Unfortunately, for salesmen the number of *"No's"* is staggering. You may encounter eight to ten *"No's"* for every one yes. It just comes with the territory.

As mentioned earlier, as a Financial Advisor I would make 100 cold calls per day to book 18 appointments (including walk-ins and referrals) each week, with 15 kept appointments to try to close. I would close seven to nine appointments the first time and close an additional two to three sales from subsequent meetings.

All *"No's"* are hard to overcome. So be prepared. You will hear it. Stay smart and become numb to the fact that someone has uttered those negative words. If turned around, a *"No"* can become one of your best sales ever.

Remember; never take the word "no" personally. Remove all negative thoughts you may have had with that word and check your ego at the door. Not all *"No's"* mean *"No."* There are various types or levels when it comes to this word *"No."* For instance there's:

- The "no," not right now.
- The "no," I'm just looking.
- The "no," I already have xyz.
- The "no," maybe next time, at least I know you have it.
- The "no," I'm not interested. With these types of no's I recommend accepting and moving on, possibly they may eventually come around!

Each of these examples, and there are many more, may have different meanings:

- One may mean, give me a moment to look around.
- The other may say, show me or tell me what you have.

Or, it could simply mean the exact meaning of the word, with the full intention of that word *"NO."* There are other prospects out there that will appreciate your time and efforts.

I look at *"No's"* very differently than most others. I look at *"No's"* as an opportunity, a challenge. It gives me a chance to do a better job in servicing/enticing the customer. Perhaps, I didn't do a good enough job at fact finding. Maybe, I need to discover a better way of presenting what we have to offer. Nevertheless, this now gives me something to work on in preparation for the next opportunity.

Regardless of the outcome, you must remember not to take *"No's"* personally. Not everyone will buy from you and there are various reasons as to why.

The Close

Close: To bring to an end; finish, to complete or make final.

For the great majority of salespeople it is believed that the *close* is the final step in the sales process. For the most part, this belief is correct. However, the *close* is an ongoing process. Asking for the sale is not only intricate, it is necessary to complete the sales process.

More importantly, the process of trying to *close* is to take place throughout the entire sales interaction. During your initial introduction you should be closing, halfway through your transaction you should be closing, and upon completing the presentation you should be closing. After the sale, during follow-ups or when asking for referrals and additional business, you should be closing.

Attempting to close (ATC) from the very onset, will help you determine whether or not you have an interested buyer. Attempting to close, establishes the customer/salesperson relationship. It clearly indicates why you are there (to make a sale).

Every step of the way, you will need to *attempt to close* the sale. After a few questions, perhaps after presenting a few of the products and their features, you should *attempt to close*. Upon covering many of the aspects of the products or services, such as, benefits, sizes, colors and or brands, you should also *attempt to close*.

You may be surprised, as to how many times you may have to attempt to close, before a customer actually bites. The closing process is not easy. You will have to determine when to make the initial attempt to close, at what intervals, and when to quit. I normally attempt to close at least four times. Should they not buy, I never take it personally.

"The close is where you begin to enjoy the fruits of your labor."

Technique in action

Speaking of *technique in action;* I can't help but think of when I first became a Financial Advisor (FA) for a local bank in the South Suburb of Chicago. I met a young banker named Brian. This young man understood the sales concept and strategies as well as any sales person twice his age. If I remember correctly, he was around 19 years of age and already being considered for a branch manager's position by the bank President.

I would visit his branch once a week for appointments and use the opportunity to go over new sales techniques and approaches I may have learned. He would listen to what I had to say without interruption. Once we were done, he would look for the very first opportunity to demonstrate what we talked about. He was good!

It was on one of the rare occasions, when I was at his branch with no set appointments. I was able to observe him opening an account with a customer. It was during this transaction that I began to understand and realize why this young man was being considered for management.

The customer was opening up several new accounts. Brian had offered her the entire array of products and services the bank was offering at that time. When it came down to offering his final product, I had seen many of his colleagues offer this simple product time and time again and watched them have it rejected time after time. So much so, that many of the other bankers refused to offer it, and subsequently scored low on their monthly review.

This final offer was for a visa/master debit card (those cards that are tied to ones checking or savings account). Instead of him asking the customer whether she wanted it or not, Brian simply asked; "Would you like one or two debit cards for ease and convenience when accessing your funds?"

The customer looked up, and said "Why would I need two of them, aren't they the same?" He went on to explain that they are for the same account. However, they had different account numbers and, that one would be for her and the other for her spouse. The customer said "No, one would be enough, and my husband doesn't care about this banking stuff."

He had found the secret to successfully overcoming an objection before it ever arose. In this instance, the customer's rejection was on the quantity, not the offer.

All great negotiators know to get what you want, you must ask for more than you expect.

This was a perfect example of one's true *desire* to overcome seeming obstacles and one's true *belief* that they are capable of getting it done. I am sure he was very much aware of the difficulties of offering these products. I am sure he was quite familiar with the struggles and concerns of his colleagues. Furthermore, I am sure he was also aware of the problem when offering the product to customers.

Based on what I witnessed, he was prepared for the very opportunity to present this in such a way that he would be certain to meet his objective.

"Preparation met with opportunity, should never be considered luck."

His preparedness is a testament to all of those who envision achieving and receiving their heart's desires. He created a script and stuck to it.

"The key to success is — Versitility; the meaning of knowledge & transformation through application"

--Jane Eller,
Former employee, Friend

KEY TO SUCCESS

"The key to success is – **Versi***tility;* (obviously a play on the spelling using my name) this was told to me by one of my former employees named Jane. She mentioned this to me on the very day that I was shutting down one of my cellular phone accessory locations. Jane and I had worked together for two years. We knew one another well, and she knew that this day was a difficult day for me, as well as for her but, it was time for us to move on.

What was so touching for me, about hearing this from her, was the fact that she told me, "Versie, I get it. I may not have used all that you have taught me but, when I did apply it, it worked and it's not about what you know, it's about application. "Knowing, what to do means nothing if you don't apply it." "Versie, I get it!" Hearing her say that meant so much to me; to have someone see my efforts and appreciate all that we shared.

The key to any successful sales position or entrepreneurial endeavor is a positive mental attitude (also known as PMA) and applied application. You must be hopeful at all times, even when others and your situation appear hopeless. You must *believe* in who you are and what you are doing. This belief will certainly go far beyond most individual's visual or mental comprehension. Unfortunately, for many people "seeing is believing."

For those of us who have *faith,* and a true *desire* to achieve, know that you must first *"believe in order to see!"*

Envisioning the future is far beyond your current situation or circumstance. This happened for *Sam Walton, founder of Sam's Club and Wal-Mart.* It happened for *Phil Jackson, head coach and ten (10) times NBA title playoff winner,* and has happened for countless others.

The ability to see beyond the present transforms your beliefs. It will take you further than any formal education, further than any physical or mental competence and further than any social associations or status.

After having discovered the knowledge needed to *transform* your life, you must know how to *apply* the *concepts, principles* and *techniques* that will allow you to become triumphant. These are many of the things that I have discussed throughout this book and, more importantly, it is what's already in your heart and your mind. "You have what it takes to be great!"

I challenge each and every one of you reading this book, to *believe. Believe* in yourself, *believe* in others, and *believe that* you can control your destiny, thereby, changing your life for the better. *"You must move towards your faith base and act upon your belief system, in order to change your circumstances."*

"I've loved the life I lived, and lived the life I loved."

--James Hopkins,
Grandfather (1913-1981)

Living the Life You Love

Many of you may not be currently *"living the life that you love"* but I am confident that you will soon be *"loving the new life that you are about to lead."* As you begin to develop a renewed sense of purpose, and a new perspective on your current life, things will begin to reveal themselves to you. Wait and see!

I've found that once you pledge to the universe your heart's true desires, gradually those things and the people once looked for appear to help you in fulfilling those desires. Suddenly, these resources begin to align themselves with you to assist in carrying out those wishes.

You may or may not be familiar with the story of the "Acres of Diamonds," told by Russell Conwell. The story has been told thousands of times and it goes something like this. There was an old farmer that was said to be financially well-off, when one day he heard that people were migrating to Africa, where they were finding diamonds and becoming rich because of them. The farmer decided to sell his farm, all his worldly possessions and head off to Africa in search of his riches.

Months later, a trader was in town when he happened upon the farm and inquired about the old farmer. The new owner informed him of what happened with the old farmer and explained that he was the new owner.

Prior to leaving, the trader asked the new owner for a drink of water. As he was waiting, he noticed a large stone on the mantel and said that's a diamond! Has the old farmer returned? The new farmer said no that's just a stone that I found one day while watering the mule by the stream. The trader said no that's a diamond in its rough form. The trader asked the farmer if he would take him to the very place where he found it. So, he did. Upon reaching the very spot where the farmer found the stone, the trader began to look around and found another and another more beautiful stone than the one before it. They had discovered that there were acres of diamonds. He said that the old farmer sold his land and traveled hundreds of miles across the country looking for *"Diamonds"* and here they were "Acres *of Diamonds"* right under his nose all the time. He just didn't know what to look for.

Are you too preoccupied with looking elsewhere for your riches that you are missing the *"Acres of Diamonds"* right there in your midst?

Sales or Service

Sales or service; soon they will no longer be viewed as two separate, stand along entities. We will all come to understand the new motto for the 21st Century as "Sales plus Service." Much like the *"Acres of Diamonds"* story this concept of sales and service is not new. It has just fallen by the way side, and individuals have forgotten that sales must be accompanied by service, in order to have continued sales.

We have all become so accustomed to buying something and, if it no longer works, trying to take it back. If you couldn't take it back, then throw it away, never mind servicing it. No more will there be the days of sales without concern for service.

Given the current financial situation there is an increasing demand for servicing.

People are shopping and spending less on new items. Be it clothes, furniture, homes or automobiles. The consumers are deciding to hold on to what they have and maintain those items. There will soon be huge increases in claims, as well as the purchasing of extended warranties and protection plans. This will help consumers not only justify any new purchases. But also, offset the potential cost of damaged or broken goods.

"Sales and service are and shall always be as one forevermore."

During the late 1800's and the early 1900's, the two went hand-in-hand. Merchants and manufacturers understood that you could not have one without the other. In fact, having them both hand-in-hand sold more products and created brand loyalty.

Servicing for many businesses, especially the automobile industry, was a very important part of the sales and service relationship. For many of these businesses, the servicing aspect of their company provided a large portion of their revenue. These business owners understood that without this servicing component, their business could not grow. With the advent of internet based sales, it left the consumer longing for the face-to-face interaction and the service portion of the transaction that only the old brick and mortar businesses could provide.

The same can be said for another service that is starting to resurface these days, "Layaway." Yes, I said it and I meant it "Layaway," "Layaway," "Layaway." Layaways are the services of retail stores that allowed mid to low income earners to have what others could afford to buy immediately.

Layaways allowed individuals to buy these same items with as little as 10% down and subsequent payments over time. What merchants forgot is that layaways brought consumers back to their stores more frequently, thereby making additional purchases, hence, placing more items on layaway. Layaways are on their way back. So, be on the lookout!

Quality of Service

It is hard to accurately describe what is considered to be good or great service. What's thought to be great to one person may be considered basic or expected by another.

There have been numerous arguments and debates surrounding this very topic. The discussion of what is good service varies greatly from individual to individual.

If you were to survey 100 people and have each of them describe what they considered to be good service, you will find this process painful and more difficult as you ask for specifics. You will see that there are 100 plus vague answers.

For instance: is it the way the Chef at a particular restaurant comes out and greets everyone? Or, is it the way the receptionist at your doctor's office smiles and gives your child a sticker? Or, could it be the way the service center at your dealership sends out those friendly maintenance reminders?

Just what is it that draws us in to a certain feeling of exhilaration with certain places, people, and things? Tell me what it is. Is it how your barber, who after 15 years, still remembers your kids' names and hasn't forgotten how you like your hair cut?

There's not one right or wrong answer to this age old question. We just seem to know good or great service. Once we've had the distinct pleasure of receiving it, it is memorable and worthwhile.

As for good service, bad service has a lasting effect on a person's psychological point of view. People can't seem to forget when they've experienced poor or bad service and they have a very long memory.

Unfortunately, with bad service, there are a lot of negative connotations to describe one's thoughts and feelings towards this type of service. Such as:

Poor	*Woeful*	*Appalling*
Bad	*Sad*	*Dreadful*
Unacceptable	*Deplorable*	*Hopeless*
Lamentable	*Inexcusable*	*Despicable*
Regrettable	*Terrible*	*Disappointing*

Are you familiar with any of these words? Have you said many of these words yourself? More importantly, are others saying these very words about you and your quality of service?

Poor and bad service is counter-productive. They could prove fatal to any business or individual. Once there is a reputation of this kind, it is difficult to change one's mind. It has been said, for every lost sale, due to bad or poor service, you must find three to five new customers to offset the one that was lost.

If bad service is due in part to low morale, bad attitude, lack of training, or low self-esteem, I strongly urge you to remedy that which is causing the problem, immediately! Bad attitudes are cancerous, running rampant through the work place, wrecking havoc on each and everyone it encounters, spreading like wildfire, and leaving a trail of victims in its path. Once encountered, every aspect of your personal and professional live is likely to be affected.

Neither low morale nor low self-esteem has any business in the work place and often is an underlining product of a deeply rooted problem. I have found that a stable personal life will duplicate itself in your professional life.

If you are having a bad day or had a fight with a significant other, keep it to yourself. The customers are not deserving of your negative attitude. They're only deserving of greatness, your 100% best. Perhaps if you can't fabricate this, you should remove yourself.

*"Excuses distract you from your goals.
Goals are the keys to success."*

*Jasmine
Student, Daughter*

GOAL SETTING

What goals did you have when you were younger? Who did you want to be when you grew up? Yes, I asked who, not what! Who was it? Was it the bus driver in your neighborhood? Was it the science teacher from your grammar school? Who?

For me, it was two people or two personas that interested me, beyond any others. The first one was the character of "Author Herbert Fonzarelli ('the *Fonz'*)," *of the TV series "Happy Days," played by Henry Winkler*. The second was "James Bond." It did not matter which "Bond." I just wanted to be either one of these characters. Not so much to really become either one of these characters, as much as I wanted to be what they each represented and to one day be able to say, "my name is Walker; Versie Walker."

For me, they were the personification of the quintessential male. Each of them was charismatic, flamboyant, powerful, and strong. Each of these gentlemen had a certain air of confidence about them. Each had power over others. The most awe inspiring characteristics of the two were their ability to command an audience.

This power that I speak of was communicated very effectively on screen and without force. People seemed to be empowered by their presence and they never abused that power. They seemed to be able to predict each situation and predict their outcome (always favorable, at least for them). For me and many others, they were *"it."* The *"it"* we all want to have and to be. Believe it or not we all do have *"it."* The same *"it"* as does a Tiger Woods, Ben Affleck, or an Oprah Winfrey, and even the Pope. We just haven't discovered how to call *"it"* into existence.

Years ago, there was a commercial for a financial services company. No matter where the commercial was set, it always had two individuals talking to one another. One would say "My advisor E.F. Hutton said..."but, before they could complete their statement, everyone within hearing distance would stop and lean in to listen, at which time the narrator would say, "When E.F. Hutton speaks, everyone listens."

To be able to command such reverence is power. Remember, you too possess these same capabilities.

I discovered some time ago that, when I began to set goals and became deliberate with my actions and exact with my words, I no longer had to "yell" or "scream" in order for people to listen. I could "simply whisper" and people would strain to hear what I was going to say. Once I began to put my words into actions, people were more willing to hear what I was trying to say and to act upon my suggestions.

Become accustomed to goal setting, and avoid excuses. Set both personal and professional goals.

You should set:

- Daily goals; (Morning, Noon, and Night)
- Weekly goals
- Monthly goals

You should hold yourself accountable for their achievements and completion. Whatever items that are not completed for a given day should roll over to the next and whatever goals that are not completed for any given week should roll over to the month.

There should be no goals that have rolled over from daily or weekly goals into a monthly goal, which extends beyond that month. Have all goals completed in the month in which they were created. Keep each new month new! This is important in order to maintain goals.

For those of you who are employed, I recommend using your employers' goals as a spring board for setting your own goals. Understand your employer's goals are the minimum requirements that they will allow, in order to achieve the company's overall objective. Remember the word <u>minimum</u>!

State your goals, outside of your employers, and outline your minimum requirements. This will enable you to meet personal and professional goals and objectives.

These goals may not necessarily be elaborate at first. They may be as simple as:

- Remembering to tell your mate how much you appreciate them.
- Owning a new home
- Vacations

- Working from home on Fridays
- Treating yourself to the Spa once in a while

Whatever your goal, set it and be sure to achieve it.

It has always puzzled me how someone such as myself, who has struggled with maintaining their weight for years. After making the decision and perhaps the commitment to lose the weight, would in the same breath discount their efforts before they would even begin. They would say things like:

- I want to lose weight but, I always seem to fail.
- I don't want to lose too much…I don't want to look sick.

Now, for the great majority of these individuals, they are and have been overweight for quite some time. Given the fact that, most Americans are largely over weight. For many of them, they would probably have to lose about 100 lbs or more too ever look sick.

It is this type of defeatist attitude that has the great majority of us up and down on yo-yo diets and never losing any weight.

As for me, when I decided and prayed for weight loss, I believed that I would lose whatever amount of weight it would take to keep me healthy. My weight began to come off and for the most part stayed off.

I did not only hope and desire but, I placed faith and belief in myself that I could get it done. I had to modify my eating habits, start an exercise routine and changed those around me. I began to take better control of my emotions and most importantly, my state of mind. Once I did these things, I experienced success.

We must do more than just praying for and hoping for a better life or better circumstances. We must desire it and have the faith and a belief system that we can create better situations for ourselves.

Begin to use positive affirmations throughout your day. This will enable you to bring forth positive outcomes in your life.

Start with something as simple as this:

- I feel great.
- I am wonderful.
- I am a good sales person.
- I will accomplish all that I desire.
- I shall be the best ever.
- I will accept the challenge and become victorious.
- I will receive prosperity in abundance.

There are a million more statements that you can add to this list. Use this list daily, say these things out loud, as you eat breakfast, as you drive to work, or as you lie in bed each night before you go to sleep.

I recommend that you set goals, and behave and live your life in accordance with the words you would like to have heard. It's been said, "People believe all of what they see and none of what they hear."

Remember *"you are who you say you are and you will be what you say you'll be"*...do not short change yourself. A new life is awaiting you!

Establish upfront that you are doing these things for yourself. They should be for you and you only. Be selfish. Goal setting changes your attitude, your life style, eating habits, and all of the toxic nonproductive things that may be suffocating you. It allows you the freedom to breathe!

Conversely, you will be giving back to the world a new you and, all those around you will benefit from the "new" you. They will and should greatly appreciate the prominence that you will display and they will begin to express it. Say proudly to yourself, "this one is for me!"

Drivers

What are your drivers? What stimulates you? What sets you into motion? Is it money or shelter? Is it fame, prestige, or status? Or, is it sex and power? What are they? Are you familiar with these drivers? Have you written them down? Do they provide any benefits? What are you willing to sacrifice to acquire them and are they healthy?

Be very careful with material and status drivers because once you have attained them, they may not be replaceable. You may experience a sense of loss. For many, this sense of loss could create an adverse effect of what their initial drivers were supposed to do.

Whatever your reasons for doing all that you do place them in the forefront of your sites. Be sure to keep them close to your heart. When you get close to the fulfillment of your heart's desires, you'll find that things will appear to get more difficult. You may feel like you want to quit or, begin to question whether all you have done is worth it. Be encouraged; stay inspired!

It is during these times you will need to hold on tighter to your faith and to refer back to these drivers to keep you focused. It is often when we get closer to our break through(s) that things appear to become tougher. That is how you know that you are close to having a break through. Keep pressing forward, don't give up!

Small Business Owners

As a former small business owner myself, I am very familiar with the challenges of owning and growing a business. One of the reasons many small businesses stay small is their inability to stay competitive in today's market place. Pricing, merchandising, marketing or purely not thinking outside the box are obstacles to overcome.

Often business owners and their sales team believe having more products to sell and lowering their prices will yield more in sales.

This strategy is not true. Lower prices mean you will work harder and receive less in revenue. Continually lowering your prices in hope of increasing sales can be a bad move. You will move more units but you will gain less revenue. When prices are too low customers will become skeptical about buying from you. They may even feel that your products are inferior.

Consider setting sales goals, and investing in smart sales people is one approach. Hire people who are creative and think outside the box. Having total product knowledge, features, and benefits coupled with a personable attitude can be the answer to not reducing your sale price. Believe that your knowledge and time is worth the cost and instill this in your sales team.

Imagine this: people place reservations for popular exclusive restaurant months in advance. They arrive early and still have to wait two or more hours for the privilege to be seated. This is a clear case of selling the "sizzle not the steak." This is the technique of making a person want the item, product, service or the mere privilege so badly that cost is of no concern. "They will justify to all others why it is worth it." Being the first, the only or part of an exclusive club is empowering and people will do whatever it takes to become a member.

Your pricing should be competitive for the market place in which you serve. Moreover, your salesperson should place more emphasis on the benefits of the product or service and not the cost. For peace of mind and convenience, people will pay an arm and a leg.

If you don't believe this, just be up at 2 a.m. and watch all the infomercials selling tons of quick fix products around the world and you will soon become a believer.

Even my family's Dentist has a strong and brilliant sales team. Every time we go to his office they are selling products, services and various cosmetic procedures... all at a dentist's office. This is a great example of "up selling" although it's a dentist office.

For all you business owners and sales managers, you may have a sales team that believes they cannot be competitive unless items are on sale or with a deep discount.

Sometimes you have greater issues than competition. You have a human resource problem. Adjust your sales staff's mindset to see the tremendous opportunity before them. If they are unable to see the benefits then they are toxic and you must rid yourself of them. Perhaps these individuals lack self-esteem, knowledge, selling skills or creativity. Whatever the problem, it is now your problem and it may kill your business!

•

"Goals are but limited dreams."

-Kendall/Daughter,
Student, Jr. Editor,

DREAMS

"Goals are but limited dreams," this was said to me by my 12 year old daughter, right after she asked me if I had decided on how many pages my book *Success, How I Ended Up Here* would be. I told her that I had set a goal of 125 pages or so and that's when she stated that *"Goals are but limited dreams."*

Her statement could have come about because of what one of her teachers told her or due to her disappointment with the number of pages that I had targeted. Either way, I was shocked and uncertain. However, I found this statement both compelling and quite difficult for a response. I had no rational comeback that could dispute or confirm her notion.

It would be two days later while preparing breakfast that it dawned on me to revisit our conversation. I watched my daughter struggle while putting butter on some biscuits. She complained that she could not do it because they were too hot. I then grabbed several of those hot biscuits and opened them up and told her that she must move beyond her temporary pain or discomfort, especially if she were ever to enjoy the pleasure of those biscuits.

It was at the breakfast table that I asked her to repeat what she had told me days earlier and she gladly did.

Thinking back on the situation with the hot biscuits and repeating her statement of *"goals are but limited dreams."* I then said to her, if that is true, then, *"excuses are the erasers of those dreams."*

I asked, "what if Steve Jobs had a dream of making the IPod, but no 'goal' of when he would produce it?" Millions of individuals would not have the pleasure of this product. Or what if Beyoncé (her favorite artist) had a dream of making a record, but no "goal" on when she would release it? Then millions of people, including her, would not have the pleasure of hearing her voice.

I encourage her and all of you reading this book to not subscribe to the philosophy that *"goals are but limited dreams."* Perhaps, goals are the very *"rails"* that dreams must travel on in order to see your dreams come to fruition.

Goals are the tracking device that follow the progression of one's dreams and enables their true desires to come forth.

For, without definite accountable goals, we could all rest on the "excuse" that our dreams are still in the developmental phase (months and years later). Without any responsibility or accountability on the part of the dreamer, then they would have no reason to ever bring their dreams to physical manifestation.

I am so glad that the Wright brothers didn't feel that their *"goals"* of taking flight were all but limited dreams. I am also glad that Barack Obama didn't believe that his *"goal"* of being the first African-American president of the United States of America, was but a limited dream. Instead he continued to believe in his *"goal"* of how he would make his dream a reality.

I thank each and every one of those individuals for dreaming and setting *"goals,"* because they have helped many of us fulfill our dreams.

Success by Example

The success I spoke of that the banker Brian experienced with his customer and the *feel, felt, found* method I described in earlier chapters. Bring to mind a pleasurable buying experience I once had.

While living in Bel Air, Maryland, I entered into a car dealership. Understand, when I entered this dealership I was *"just looking"* and *"not interested in anything particular."* I was immediately met by a salesman by the name of David, an older gentleman, with a soft spoken voice. He was recently retired and worked there for a few months to keep him busy.

After browsing the show room, he invited me to test drive one of their new SUVs, the Sequoia; I accepted. He took the owner's new fully equipped all white SUV. Shortly after we drove off, David began to ask a series of questions (very informal and none imposing). He asked, not what I liked about the vehicle, but what things that I did not like and what would I take away from this nicely equipped vehicle.

Obviously, after sitting in this luxurious SUV, there wasn't much that I wanted to take away from it. He then asked if I would buy or lease and what figure would they need to come up with in order for me to drive a car away that day. I gave him some outrageous numbers because, I was *"just looking"* and *"not interested in anything particular."*

He asked a few more questions regarding my career, my family, and what brought us to the area. Then, he asked one strange question, did I have a garage or did I park on the street. As a homeowner with a new house built from the ground, I answered him very proudly, A garage of course.

David then asked, "Do you think that this truck will fit in your garage, because, as you know, we may be able to meet your criteria in case you were no longer *'just looking'.*" He stated that all of our discussions could be a waste of time if the vehicle couldn't fit into my garage and he then said "Mr. Walker, you do like this vehicle, right." I said "yes." "Would you like to go by the house to see if it would fit," he asked. I replied "most certainly," and then I hit the gas pedal.

Now, all of his idle chatter and non essential fact finding was ultimately used against me, back at his office along with the aid of my wife. When I tried every excuse not to buy, he would so eloquently remind me that "Mr. Walker you did say X," I would say yes. Then, he would say, but, "Mr. Walker we are able to do Y" and with my wife on his side, what was a guy to do besides signing on the dotted line.

This was one of the most professional and pleasurable car buying experiences I had ever had. However, I walked away with more than a new car, and a new car payment. I walked away with a wonderful experience, and a new technique of fact finding and closing sales.

Sales are much like answering the phone. You can respond to questions when you are ready, especially now with caller ID. You can get a little information before you pick up the phone. I recommend using the same technique when handling customers' questions. Find out a little bit about the customer. Discover their styles and buying habits. Next time instead of rushing to answer their question, such as how much something may cost, simply restate the question or hesitate to answer as you are attempting to get the item or to ask them another question.

By doing so, you allow yourself time to think through the question and think through your response. Always maintain control.

Being Sold

No one wants to be sold! Customers want to have a trained professional show them a variety or a variation of the products that are suitable for their needs. At which time, they can make an informed decision based on those facts.

People resent items or products being forced down their throats. They do, however, appreciate a person who will ask specific questions that will help lead them to a buying decision. This is the very reason that personal sales will never be entirely lost to infomercials or the internet online sales. People still look for and desire that personal touch.

I cannot stress how human interaction cements the selling process. People look for some interaction during the sales process, however slight the gesture may be. This gives everyone a sense of purpose and belonging. There have been customers and sales people alike that have said, replacing the human element with automated phone service or self service centers, takes away from the necessary sales process.

Decision makers

As a Financial Advisor, when setting appointments, I would always ask to meet with all of the decision makers, even if they were not named on the particular asset that we would be reviewing. This was so important to closing the deal that, if an appointment showed up without their mate, I would pretend to have just received an emergency call that I must run to and ask if we could reschedule our appointment. It took some time to develop this habit.

After setting 15 or so appointments each week half would show up without their spouse. If I still went ahead with the meeting I was told I'll take this back to the Mrs. and one of us will get back to you. But I would never hear from them again. Some had taken the information and went elsewhere to purchase what I had recommended. *"Time is money and time wasted is just that, wasted time."*

Once I began to implement this new structure, my "NO shows" dropped significantly and my closing ratio increased dramatically.

One thing I strongly recommend doing is what all of the top business professionals are doing today. From doctors' offices to attorneys' offices, they are all calling their appointments a day or so ahead of their scheduled appointment time, confirming that the appointment will be kept. This serves several purposes, one, as a courtesy call. Two, it places the person on notice of the appointment. Three it lets you know how to schedule or adjust your day. Further, it lets the customer know indirectly, that your time is valuable and if they have no intention of showing up, to let you know right away.

If you sense any hesitation by the customer, you can feel free to tell them that you have a tight schedule and, if they are not interested, that you could perhaps place someone else in their time slot. This is effective, especially if you noticed that they either no-show a lot or frequently call to cancel.

You should set a personal *"no show"* and cancellation threshold, for me it was three. You had three times to do any combination of the above mentioned. I then no longer considered them as a viable prospect and placed them in my three to six month follow-up folder.

Mentioning decision makers, reminds me of working at my cell phone accessory stores. Cell phone accessories attract the young and old alike. Many times, parents would be at the mall with their children, shopping and spending quality time.

On many occasions, they would walk past one of our locations. At times, the parents were just as enthused as the kids were about our products and other times they simply were not. This could have been for any number of reasons: tired, running late, hungry, or just ready to go.

In the beginning, I was eager to make a sale, so much so that, I was unaware or would totally ignore the fact that the parent wasn't in the buying mood. There were many instances, where this cost me the loss of a sale. The parental body would say "no, let's go," or "I told you nothing else, I have spent enough on you," or even "I don't think you need anything else." This had become very concerning to me, until one day I decided to pay attention to the parents and engage them throughout the sales process.

There was one time in particular, when this teenage girl and her mom approached our location (much to her daughter's urging). As the girl was looking over several items that I had pointed out, I noticed that her mother was removed from what we were doing, with arms folded and eyes staring off into the distance.

I immediately turned to the mom and asked "*is this your baby girl,*" or "*your only?*" With arms still folded, slightly smiling, she looked at me and answered "Yes, she is my only baby" and "she is working my nerves." I then said I see that she is "*spoiled*" and "*I bet that you wouldn't have it any other way.*" She then unfolded her arms and said "You are right," at which time her daughter asked "Mom, which one do you think I should get?" I paused, and to my surprise, instead of her mother saying some of the things I mentioned earlier, she said "Well, I don't like any of them, but if you are going to get either one, I would go with the red one."

I was floored. My plan worked beautifully and continued to work each and every time. The mom did not veto my sale. She actually co-signed on it, with those sweet words "if you are going to get either one, I would go with the red one." From that moment on I engaged everyone that approached our locations, warm and friendly...

These slight adjustments in my sales approach increased my sales and repeat business 100%. It was hard to imagine. Could this be one of the keys that you are missing, thereby prohibiting you from being successful?

Many times the initial person making the inquiry didn't even buy but, by engaging or acknowledging the other person(s) with them, this led to other sales opportunities.

The Big Competitor's Disadvantage

While working in the cell phone accessory industry, I'd watch day in and day out how the large cellular phone carriers would miss and blow huge opportunities.

Many of the major players, Verizon, AT&T, T-Mobile, etc., would train their staff to seek out customers for new phone service, but, they would miss the ball entirely when offering cellular accessories.

When it comes down to offering cellular accessories, these guys have a captive audience. Truth be told, they had a great advantage over companies such as mine. They could buy in bulk, they could market this product through various media outlets, they were able to bundle any of these items as they saw fit, and lastly, they had the customers first. I know many of the cell phone accessory stores that would kill for such an opportunity. Honestly, many of them over looked the obvious sales as well.

These companies and their employees were so oblivious to many of these opportunities that, often times they wouldn't even view me as a threat to their business.

For the most part, they were unaware of the variety of products that we offered. Many times, we would offer the exact same product (manufacture and packaging) as they would, for 50 to 75% less than they did. I had access to the same distributors and venders. I would wave and speak to each of their employees on a daily basis and on several occasions explain to them that we were not in competition with them. We only filled a void that they cared not to service. We serviced a segment of the market that they were not interested in.

I further explained that they handle newer customers with newer phones, whereby we focused primarily on the older phone models. Contrary to that statement, we actually sold accessories for the older models as well as the most recent ones. We carried everything from face plates to chargers, antennas, Bluetooth's, memory cards, batteries and did I mention IPod accessories?

On rare occasions, when the major competitors knew that we were soliciting their customers, based on our constant professional and personal customer service style, they still could not defend against our progressive sales approach.

Many times, these same employees would advise their customers against purchasing products from shops like ours even though they would secretly buy from us themselves. When they were out of certain items, they sometimes would direct customers our way.

These cellular carriers would even advise their customers to go outside the mall in search of what they needed or search the web in hopes of discouraging them from buying from us. I have personally witnessed many of these employees telling customers that products for their particular phones were no longer available (bad business); just to get the customers to buy a new phone; thus, locking the customer into a new phone plan, when a new battery or charger could have fixed their problem.

After witnessing these types of tactics, I decided to make certain that every customer, who walked passed one of our locations, would be aware of all that was available for their model phone. The competitors' customers would be heard talking about how refreshing it was to have a place like ours. Also, that we not only had what they needed but, we were also knowledgeable of cell phones.

Here recently, several of these major cell phone carriers have come to realize that cellular accessories are a big business and could account for a large part of their overall revenue. One company in particular (Verizon) has gone so far as to carry colorful and trendy accessories and giving many of these items away for free with new account activation. It has been said that some of the cell phone carriers have informed their employees that, if they are seen talking to any of the competitors, they risk losing their jobs.

Missed Opportunities

There have been many times that I've missed out on some great opportunities (yes, even me). Once, after selling a customer a car charger, I saw the same customer some time later, with a bag from Radio Shack. I called him over to me and was able to see inside his bag. I saw that he had a particular Bluetooth inside. I said to him, "you bought that from there, I sell those," and he looked at me very sheepishly and said "I didn't know." "I would have bought it from you."

Sometime later, after no longer being angry, I came to realize that it was not his fault, it was mine. I hadn't shared with him all the various products that we made available to our customers. It didn't happen again. I sang out for all to hear what we offered. Literally!

Speaking of, *missed opportunities*. One of the malls that we were located in on the West Coast sat an ice cream shop just 30 feet away from our location. I had been attempting to get the attention of one of their customers. This lady was actively talking to someone on her phone. When all of a sudden, she began to fumble with the phone; her child and the ice cream cone she was holding. The ice cream cone fell and she nearly dropped her phone. One of my employees jumped into action, she grabbed several sheets of our paper towels and proceeded to help the lady clean up the mess.

After it was over, the lady said her thanks and my employee was feeling good for being able to assist her. Meanwhile, this employee never mentioned to the lady how this time it was only her ice cream cone and how it could have been her cell phone and that next time she might not be so fortunate. This employee made no suggestion to the lady about coming over and seeing what was available, to help protect her investment. Big mistake, huge missed opportunity!

Being Up For the Challenge

I mentioned earlier the home my wife and I built in New York, and how I took my kids by, day after day, showing them their rooms and mentioning the fact that we had not yet secured financing.

About eleven months earlier, we were building our first home together in Bel Air, Maryland. Shortly after my wife started her new job, we had two relocation offers presented to us.

Prior to the construction, we owned property but had never built before. We were faced with a lot of obstacles. Relocating, new schools for our kids, learning a new area (being homesick), and hand selecting every single item to go into the home (I mean everything).

We struggled to get decent interest rates, due in part to the size of the loan. Most of the banks were considering the size of the loan to be what they termed as a *"Jumbo Loan"* at that time, anything over $300,000. The difficulty with this was not only the increased rate but also the amount of money required as a down payment.

I had taken on the task of seeking out competitive rates from various banks. We had one large national home lender that was willing to finance us, with a high interest rate. With our closing date nearing, I became uncomfortable with their terms, their rates, and the fact that our loan would be sold to another lender within six months.

Sitting in my office at work one day, with just 18 days left to close, I wasn't feeling confident as to what we were about to do, when I decided to call my former boss and friend Jerry McCarthy, to see how he was doing. When I called, he wasn't in, but his long-time love, Alanna was there. She and I talked for quite some time. We talked about our industry, about my kids and about our move. At this point, I began telling her about our financing concerns; she listened and then gave me one piece of advice, she said *"Don't give up."*

After speaking with her, I became reenergized, refocused and set out on a new mission. I got out the yellow pages for the area and found four banks in our area. I called each of them. Two of the banks said they could handle our loan but they would need 30 days or so, one said maybe they could but they would need 25 days for the turnaround (not including the weekend).

It was now 4:00 o'clock on this Thursday and not feeling very confident about all this, when I picked up the phone and called the last bank. I spoke with their loan officer, gave her all of our information, told her of our time frame (18 days including the weekends), told her that we didn't want our information or our loan to be sold and she said *"Okay, let's get it done."*

I was shocked. I called my wife and had her meet me at the bank to sit with the loan officer around 6:30 that evening.

Their rates were great, her personality was wonderful. Let me remind you that we had only 18 days till closing and they were not all business days. They were calendar days which included two weekends and one holiday.

By the following Monday, after speaking with other people and having concerns as to whether or not it were possible for her to meet our deadline, I called her back. I informed her that we were going to stay with the large national lender, because they had all our information and they could meet our deadline, thanks.

She stopped me. She assured me that she had it all together and under control. She felt that it was unfair for us to pay a higher interest rate and for our loan to then be sold, when her company was capable of handling it all in house. At that time, I decided to let her continue the process. It was her passion and conviction that allowed me to rest assured that we were in good hands.

Not only did she and her team meet our needs, they far exceeded them, they had everything done one day earlier.

Not enough can be said for thinking big. This was an enormous undertaking. Any of you, that have built or bought a home, would know. The other banks didn't feel that they were capable of meeting the task set before them and they didn't even care to try.

Furthermore, this loan officer proved to me that if you have a desire to achieve, do not let minor details, (such as time lines) or seeming obstacles divert you from your goal. See, she had no doubt that she could deliver. It was

I, who let doubt seep in and she immediately laid them all to rest. That's the whole concept of positive thinking.

I am glad that I reached out to my friend in Chicago and followed his mate's advice...it brought me back to right-minded thinking.

CLOSING

In closing, I would like to say that, much like you I have had some challenges, disappointments, setbacks, and controversy and plain old fashion tough luck. Through it all, I managed to bounce back. At every crossroad, I made some tough decisions, many times more difficult than the last ones. However, I made them. After each challenge, I reinvented myself, awoken the small voice inside and then challenged myself again.

Many times, you will need to test your own vigor, your own armor, and then let the world check to see if there are any chinks in that armor.

I managed to switch careers, change industries, become self-employed, an entrepreneur, publisher, and author. Although I am not done as I travel down life's journey, I eagerly anticipate what's on the road ahead.

Take control of your life, take charge and always remember, that, "*You are and always will be the best in what you <u>choose</u> to do.*"

"Do not allow 'fear and excuses' to keep you from setting realistic and attainable goals, for I see no other way of having your dreams come true."

--Versie L. Walker,
Author, Entrepreneur, Salesman

APPENDIX

RECOMMENDED READING/BIBLIOGRAPHY

Baker, Billy. "Top Sales Career For Women." EzineArticles Submission - Submit Your Best Quality Original Articles For Massive Exposure. Ezine Publishers Get 25 Free Article Reprints. 12 Feb. 2007. 1 Feb. 2009 <http://www.ezinearticles.com/?Top-Sales-Career-For-Women&id=452371>.

Brown, Les. It's Not Over Until You Win! How to Become the Person You Always Wanted to Be No. New York: Simon and Schuster, 1997.

Brown, Les. Live Your Dreams. New York: William Marrow and company, 1992.

Bult, John. "Women and Sales Jobs." SG & Singapore Map - Singapura, Singapur, Singapore Information & Tourism. 1 Feb. 2009 <http://streetdirectory.com/travel_guide/189273/careers_and_job_hunting/women_and_sales_jobs.html>.

Covey, Stephen R. The 7 Habits of Highly Effective People. New York City: Free Press, 1990.

"Gail Devers Biography." Gail Devers Official Web Site. 1 Feb. 2009 <http://www.gaildevers.com/biography.htm>.

Halvorsen, Rob . "Top Sales Careers for Women." Sales Jobs - Sales Recruiters - Sales Careers Online. 1 Feb. 2009 <http://www.salescareersonline.com/articles/article_08022006.html>.

Hill, Napoleon, and Arthur Pell. Think and Grow Rich: The Landmark Bestseller-- Now Revised and Updated for the 21st Century. New York: Tarcher, 2005.

Hill, Napoleon. The Law of Success In Sixteen Lessons by Napoleon Hill (Complete, Unabridged). Unknown: Bnpublishing.Com, 2007.

Palubinskas, Ed S. "How to Change Free Throw
Shooting Mechanics." <u>EzineArticles
Submission - Submit Your Best Quality
Original Articles For Massive Exposure, Ezine
Publishers Get 25 Free Article Reprints</u>.
18 Dec. 2008. 1 Feb. 2009 <http://
ezinearticles.com/?How-to-Change-Free-
Throw-Shooting-Mechanics&id=1802828>.

Ransford, Marc. "Women transforming sales
into a female-dominated career." <u>Ball
State University - Home</u>. 14 May 1998. 1
Feb. 2009 <http://www.bsu.edu/news/
article/0,1370,-1019-444,00.html>.

Shomon, Mary. "Olympian Gail Devers' Thyroid
Saga." <u>Thyroid Disease Information -
Hypothyroidism - Hyperthyroidism - Thyroid
Cancer - Autoimmune Disease - Hashimoto's
- Graves' - Goiter - Nodules</u>. 3 Dec. 2003.
1 Feb. 2009 <http://thyroid.about.com/
cs/famouspeople/a/devers.htm>.

Tracy, Brian. <u>Maximum Performance Success
in America. Five Steps to Goal Setting.
(vhs)</u>. Phoenix: Brian Tracy, 2000.

Trudeau, Kevin. <u>25 Secrets to Wealth Creation
Audio CD!</u>. New York: Debt Cures, 2007.

"Unknown." <u>Wikipedia The Free Encyclopedia</u>. 1 Feb. 2009 <en.wikipedia.org/wiki/Main Page>.

World, Websters New. <u>Websters New World College Dictionary 4ED</u>. Akron: Idg Books, 1999.

<u>Negotiating For Your Life -</u>. New York: Henry Holt Publishing -, 1993.

<u>The E-Myth Revisited CD: Why Most Small Businesses Don't Work and What to do about it</u>. New York: HarperAudio, 2004.

<u>The Secret (Extended Edition)</u>. Dir. Drew Heriot. Perf. Unknown. DVD. Ts Production, Llc, 2006.

GLOSSARY

Assertive- adj. characterized by assertion; positive or confident in a persistent way

Attitude- a manner of acting, feeling, or thinking that shows one's disposition, opinion, mood, etc.

Auto-suggestion- n. suggestion to oneself arising within one's own mind and having effects on one's thinking and bodily functions (the effects can be either positive or negative).

Believe- to have trust or confidence (in) as being true, real, or good, etc. to have religious faith.

Buyer's remorse- A term used to describe when a customer purchases something and goes home (may or may not speak to someone else for conformation/ validation of the purchase); it is an emotional condition whereby a person feels remorse or regret after a purchase. It is frequently associated with the purchase of higher value items which could be considered "bad" although it may also stem from a sense of not wishing to be "wrong." In an extreme situation, an individual who struggles with or cannot accept the possibility that they may have made a mistake, may be suffering from a more serious and severe condition that has truly little to do with ""buyer's remorse." (Wikipedia)

Cold Calling- the process of approaching prospective customers or clients, typically via the telephone, who was not expecting such an inter-action. The word "cold" is used because the person receiving the call is not expecting a call or has not specifically asked to be contacted by a sales person. Cold calls can also be done in person rather than over the phone. This type of cold call is also referred to as door to door. (Wikipedia)

Competitors- n. a person who competes; rival, a business, team etc. that competes (Webster's New World College Dictionary 4th ed)

Customer Service- (also known as Client Service) is the provision of service to customers before, during and after a purchase.

According to Turban et al. (2002), **Customer Service** is a series of activities designed to enhance the level of customer satisfaction – that is, the feeling that a product or service has met the customer expectation. (Wikipedia)

Close- to bring to an end; finish, to complete or make final (Webster's New World College Dictionary 4th ed)

Creative- adj. creating or able to create, having or showing imagination and artistic or intellectual inventiveness (Webster's New World College Dictionary 4th ed)

Decisive- adj. determining or closely affecting what comes next critically important; crucial / a decisive moment in his career (Webster's New World College Dictionary 4th ed)

Desire- to wish or long for; crave covet, to ask for; request, n. a strong wish or craving, a thing or person desired. (Webster's New World College Dictionary 4th ed)

Determination- the quality of being resolute, firmness of purpose, determined (Webster's New World College Dictionary 4th ed)

Dreams- a fond hope or aspiration to think (of) as at all possible, desirable, etc (Webster's New World College Dictionary 4th ed)

Dun- to make repeated and insistent demands upon, esp. for the payment of a debt (dictionary .com)

Entrepreneur- n. a person who organizes and manages a business undertaking, assuming the risk for the sake of the profit (Webster's New World College Dictionary 4th ed)

Faith- unquestioning belief that does not require proof or evidence, complete trust, confidence, or reliance (Webster's New World College Dictionary 4th ed)

Insurance producer- is the person selling an insurance product or service (also known as an insurance agent) to someone looking to be insured against loss. (Webster's New World College Dictionary 4th ed)

Objections- n. is an exclamation of disagreement or opposition, disapproval or dislike. (Webster's New World College Dictionary 4th ed)

Order taker- type of salesperson who only collects orders but does not make any diligent attempt to find new customers, or to persuade existing customers to increase the size or frequency of their orders. (Business dictionary.com)

Phone-phobia- n. an irrational, excessive, persistent fear of cold calling (calling on unknown prospective customers); a fear of being rejected or humiliated over the phone (reluctance to cold calling), a term widely used in the insurance and telemarketing industries.

Proactive- adj. assuming an active rather than a passive, role in doing, accomplishing, etc. taking the initiative (Webster's New World College Dictionary 4th ed)

Prospect- n. a looking forward to something; anticipation, something hoped for or expected, apparent chance for success, a likely or prospective customer, candidate, undertaking, etc. (Webster's New World College Dictionary 4th ed)

Proactive- adj. assuming an active rather than a passive, role in doing, accomplishing, etc. taking the initiative (Webster's New World College Dictionary 4th ed)

Prosperous- having continued success, prospering; flourishing, well-to-do; favorable (Webster's New World College Dictionary 4th ed)

Role play(ing)- n. a technique in training or psychotherapy in which participants assume and act out roles as to resolve conflict, practice appropriate behavior for various situations, etc. (Webster's New World College Dictionary 4th ed)

Salesman- n. a man employed as a sales clerk, sales representative (Webster's New World College Dictionary 4th ed)

Sales person- n. a person employed to sell goods or services (Webster's New World College Dictionary 4th ed)

Sales pitch- (also known as scripts/talk offs) a term widely used in the sales industry, whereby someone is stating, delivering or giving their canned or stated spill (pitch) on their goods, products and or services towards a prospective buyer.

Sales promotion- the use of publicizing methods other than paid advertising to promote a product, service, etc. (Webster's New World College Dictionary 4th ed)

Sales representative- a sales person (sales rep., esp. one employed as a traveling agent for a manufacturer, etc. (Webster's New World College Dictionary 4th ed)

Sell- to give up, deliver, or exchange (property goods or services, etc.) for money or its equivalent (Webster's New World College Dictionary 4th ed)

Success- n. a favorable or satisfactory outcome or result, the gaining of wealth, fame, rank, etc (Webster's New World College Dictionary 4th ed)

Supply and demand- is an economic model based on price and quantity in a market. It predicts that in a competitive market, price will function to equalize the quantity demanded by consumers, and the quantity supplied by producers, resulting in an economic equilibrium of price and quantity. The model incorporates other factors changing equilibrium as a shift of demand and/or supply, (demand increases price rise, supply increase price falls) (Wikipedia)

Suspects- is a term used in sales when referring to someone with whom you have no knowledge or any indication that may be interested in what you have to offer, you assume that if given the opportunity to speak with or meet with them, that you could uncover a need.

Telephone solicitation- is a method of direct marketing in which a salesperson solicits to prospective customers to buy products or services, either over the phone or through a subsequent face to face or Web conferencing appointment scheduled during the call. (Wikipedia)

INDEX

About The Author

Versie L. Walker is a native of Chicago. He was raised on the near north side, surrounded by a loving family, which included his grandparents, aunts and uncles. Later, his family moved to the south side of the city.

Versie was a child of teenage parents. His mother was still in her teens, when his parents separated. Raised in a single family household was difficult. Nonetheless, his mother taught him, at an early age, the importance of hard work and the value of family and honesty.

Apart from growing up in a single family household, his childhood was fairly normal. He had his challenges and struggles. He struggled with trying to have a voice in a female dominant family. He also struggled with being accepted and even had his struggles on the playground. Versie has struggled with weight gain. He has said that he even struggled with writing this book. He was concerned with grammatical errors, spelling and wondering if his audience would appreciate its content.

During the early years of his childhood he was unaware of many of the perils that surrounded friends and neighbors. During these years, individuals believed very firmly in "it takes a village to raise a child" and a child dared not rise up against the village.

It was not until he moved to uptown (further north of the city), where he first noticed vast differences in our society. It still is the melting pot of the city. That is where he first saw the homeless, drug addicts, prostitutes and street gangs! His reality was forever altered.

Through a series of unexpected events, he decided that he wanted more from his life. He started to seek out truth principles, began demanding better answers and commanding better results for his actions and from others. Through books and a new found commitment, he took control of his life.

Versie has been in sales for more than 20 years. He has self-studied his way into various professional sales careers. Now, he is a self-employed business man and entrepreneur. His knowledge and experience, when it comes to sales, are unparalleled. He has decided, for the first time, to share with all of you, his ideas, techniques, philosophies and life experiences, in hopes of helping you find the winner inside you.

ORDER FORM

Fax the order form to: 1-888-390-0232.

Telephone orders: Call 1-877-41-A-New-U (877-412-6398) -Have your credit card ready.

Email orders: orders@NewLookPublishing.com

Postal orders: A New Look Publishing , P.O. Box 1111, New York, NY 12533-1111, USA: 1-877-41-A-New-U

Please send the following books, CD's. I understand that I may return the product for a full refund-for any reason, no questions asked.

_____

_____

Please send more FREE information on:
- o   Other Books
- o   Speaking/Seminars
- o   Consulting
- o   Mentoring Sessions

Name: _____

Address: _____

City: _____ State: _____

Telephone: _____

Email address: _____

Sales tax: Please add 8.125% for products shipped to New York addresses.

Shipping by air

U.S. $5.00 for first book or CD and $3.00 for each additional product.

International: $10.00 for first book or CD; $6.00 for each additional product (estimate).

ORDER FORM

Fax the order form to: 1-888-390-0232.

Telephone orders: Call 1-877-41-A-New-U (877-412-6398) -Have your credit card ready.

Email orders: orders@NewLookPublishing.com

Postal orders: A New Look Publishing , P.O. Box 1111, New York, NY 12533-1111, USA: 1-877-41-A-New-U

Please send the following books, CD's. I understand that I may return the product for a full refund-for any reason, no questions asked.

_____

_____

Please send more FREE information on:
- o   Other Books
- o   Speaking/Seminars
- o   Consulting
- o   Mentoring Sessions

Name: _____

Address: _____

City: _____   State: _____

Telephone: _____

Email address: _____

Sales tax: Please add 8.125% for products shipped to New York addresses.

Shipping by air

U.S. $5.00 for first book or CD and $3.00 for each additional product.

International: $10.00 for first book or CD; $6.00 for each additional product (estimate).

ORDER FORM

Fax the order form to: 1-888-390-0232.

Telephone orders: Call 1-877-41-A-New-U (877-412-6398) -Have your credit card ready.

Email orders: orders@NewLookPublishing.com

Postal orders: A New Look Publishing , P.O. Box 1111, New York, NY 12533-1111, USA: 1-877-41-A-New-U

Please send the following books, CD's. I understand that I may return the product for a full refund-for any reason, no questions asked.

_____

_____

Please send more FREE information on:
- o   Other Books
- o   Speaking/Seminars
- o   Consulting
- o   Mentoring Sessions

Name: _____

Address: _____

City: _____ State: _____

Telephone: _____

Email address: _____

Sales tax: Please add 8.125% for products shipped to New York addresses.

Shipping by air

U.S. $5.00 for first book or CD and $3.00 for each additional product.

International: $10.00 for first book or CD; $6.00 for each additional product (estimate).